History Today

History Today

Journal of the Indian History and Culture Society

No. 1 2000

Editors

Surjit Kaur Jolly **Vandana Kaushik**

D.K. Printworld (P) Ltd.
New Delhi

Cataloging in Publication Data — DK
[Courtesy: D.K. Agencies (P) Ltd. <docinfo@dkagencies.com>]

History today : journal of the Indian History and Culture Society, no. 1, 2000 / editors, Surjit Kaur Jolly, Vandana Kaushik.
viii, 85 p. 28 cm.
Reprint. Originally published: New Delhi : Indian History and Culture Society, 2000.
Includes bibliographical references.
ISBN 8124604304

1. India — History. 2. India — Civilization. 3. India — Social conditions. I. Jolly, Surjit Kaur, 1950- II. Kaushik, Vandana.

DDC 954 22

ISBN 81-246-0430-4
First Published in India in 2000
Reprinted in 2007

History Today, no. 1 (2000) **Rs. 350** **$ 25.00**

Reprint authorised by
Indian History and Culture Society, New Delhi - 110016

Manuscripts (Whether in the form of aricles or notes or book reviews) offered for publcation, should be sent to the Editor, History Today, Indian History and Culture Society, B-17, Qutab Institutional Area, New Delhi-110016.

The Editors are not responsible for the opinions expressed by the contributors.

Published and printed by:
D.K. Printworld (P) Ltd.
Regd. office : *'Sri Kunj,'* F-52, Bali Nagar
Ramesh Nagar Metro Station
New Delhi - 110 015
Phones : (011) 2545-3975, 2546-6019; *Fax* : (011) 2546-5926
E-mail : dkprintworld@vsnl.net
Web : www.dkprintworld.com

History Today

Contents

Indian History and Culture Society (Regd.)

B-17, Qutab Institutional Area, New Delhi - 110 016

Editorial

The first issue of *History Today* is in your hands. We are overwhelmed to see a dream being realised mainly due to the single-minded devotion and efforts of Dr. S.P. Gupta, the first Organising Secretary of the Indian History and Culture Society, presently Chairman, Indian Archaeological Society.

The first issue has been dedicated to the sacred memory of Professor Devahuti and Professor D.P. Singhal.This visionary couple had travelled far and wide, visiting various countries and sites of the major civilizations of the world—Egypt, Greece, Rome, China and Peru, enriching themselves and the society.

Dr. Devahuti (born May 22, 1929) did her Master in History from Punjab University. In 1956 she obtained her Doctoral Degree from the London University. She accompanied her husband to Malaya, and then to Australia, at Brisbane. She was great admirer of Indian culture. Love for India was so strong in her that she came back to serve her country. She joined Delhi University as a Reader in the Department of History and subsequently elevated to the Professorship in South campus of the same university. After the untimely demise of her husband she took up the responsibility of Director of the Centre for Research and Training in History, Archaeology and Palaeo-Environment which the couple had founded. She passed away in 1988.

Damodar Prasad Singhal graduated from Punjab University in 1946 and obtained his Master's degree in Political Science from Punjab University in 1949. After marrying Devahuti in 1950 they went to London for doctoral research. Dr. Singhal served there for some time as Political Commentator for the B.B.C. also. After obtaining his Ph.D. degree Dr. Singhal was appointed as Lecturer in the University of Malaya. Later he taught at the Queensland University in Brisbane and obtained a Professorship in 1969. In 1975 he was awarded the Degree of Doctor of Letters from the University of Queensland for his distinguished contributions. He was a Fellow of the Royal Historical Society and the Royal Asiatic Society. He was Chairman of the Indian History and Culture Society from 1982 through 1985. In 1986 he was honoured with the Presidentship of the Centre for Research and Training in History, Archaeology and Palaeo-Environment of which he himself had laid the foundation stone in New Delhi. In this very year he passed away.

Devahuti and Prof. Singhal were scholars of eminence. Both of them wrote many articles and books on Indian History and World Civilization.

Prof. Devahuti's colleagues, friends and students remember her with warm love and feel glorified to be associated with her. Her dedication to history, deep study of sources, analytical approach and a spirit of true Indian are worthy of appreciation.

Here we would like to pay our tributes to this couple who provided the much required financial support to the Society to get a piece of land measuring 1.54 acres at B-17, Qutab Institutional Area, New Delhi where the Society's headquarter is located today.

In 1978 the first conference of the Indian History and Culture Society was held at New Delhi. On this occasion a souvenir was published. It contained an introduction by Prof. Devahuti which laid down the vision of the Society. We are reproducing this Introduction so that the readers get the clear vision of the Society and an article published by Prof. D.P. Singhal in the same souvenir, since it gives the historiography of Indian history in precise terms with great insight. Prof. Lallanji Gopal of the Banaras Hindu University had sent us his long review of the book *Ancient India: In Historical Outline* by Prof. D.N. Jha which could not be published in his life time, is being published in this journal.

The *History Today* is not based on any particular line of thought or bias. The vision of this journal had in fact emerged after long deliberations amongst the founding-fathers of the Indian History and Culture Society. It is an organisation of well meaning people who want to study and understand human history with the vision of a true historian. History is neither just a dead account of the past, nor history of political events, kings and lords but one can listen the throbbing of people's heart in it. One should try to listen to those throbs, thrills, tension, challenges, achievements and performances through the sources of history. History resides in literature, manuscripts, archaeological remains, buildings and folklore, keeping in view the conditions and environment. The present issue covers a wide range of time-frame and diverse subjects, reviews of books as well as new source material.

Our endeavour is to provide a forum to historians and scholars to express their views and perceptions freely and fearlessly against all misleading, distorted and personal opinions which are very often passed on to unsuspected readership of this country as true history. We call upon every one to adhere to the rigours of our discipline in order to earn respect from our colleagues in particular and public in general. Ours is a very sacred and responsible duty because distorted history can kill a society, culture, nation and immensly harm its existence.

Dr. Surjit Kaur Jolly
Dr. Vandana Kaushik

Vision of the Indian History and Culture Society

Devahuti

HISTORY and culture encompass a very large area of intellectual activity to include multiple genres of interactive response,* from the critically controlled to the imaginative and cognitive. The widening base of education in India—a country, populous, developing and with a premium on learning in its value system—is leading to a gradual increase in the numbers of those who literally and metaphorically derive their sustenance from such activity.

Knowledge of this kind, unless regularly exposed to sympathetic and critical evaluation by its holders, both at the intimate level and at the community level, faces the dangers of inbreeding.

At this juncture in our national life when some of the basic questions about the study and writing of history are being raised, it becomes necessary to create a new forum, the Indian History and Culture Society, for a dialogue among like-minded as well as contending historians so that a consensus can be reached, no doubt to give rise to conflict and then a further consensus in a continuing process. Not only is interaction needed among historians themselves, between them and other social scientists, but also between them and those who make history—the artists, literary writers and philosophers. For it is their activity which culminates in a norm of collective action and becomes an integral part of concrete history. They are as much the makers of history as the agents of change, both in the sense of evolution and in the sense of permutation and innovation, as the mechanism of production and distribution during that age. Integrated history therefore is involved with arts, humanities and social sciences.

There is a keen need for interchange of ideas on several important subjects for which it is hoped the Society would provide opportunity through workshops and seminars. We need to discuss specific problems of immediate relevance such as India's political culture, the role of the intellectual, the rationale of Hindu communalism, the rationale of Muslim communalism, the linguistic ethos and so forth. For the study of Indian history in general we are very much in need of Indian frameworks of reference because the general becomes intelligible only through the specific, the universal through the unique.

While the different historical approaches are valid for their own time and place, they will ring true to us, if they do, in part or in whole, or not at all, only if we comprehend them in terms of our own reality and own past experience. We have to be our own *messiahs*, to feel, to understand, to interpret our own

*The interaction between facts, objects and ideas and man, their creator as well as observer and recepient.

history and fully to appreciate the validity or otherwise of the revelation of others, of the frames of refernce of others, in our context of time and place. To comprehend history we have to keep on observing the remains and reading our sources till we are able to see the objects in use and people in action. The essential matter of history is not what happened but what people thought and said about it. The essential matter of Indian history is what the Indian people, ordinary or special thought and said about events and ideas. It is that self-definition which represents the Indian feel for attitude towards and use of history even if it be the rejection of history as real, and its transmutation into myths and symbols. We will have to see what attitude they had to history and how did they apply their interpretation of it in their times—Kapila, Charvaka, Buddha, Asoka, Kalhana, Akbar, Syed Ahmad, Iqbal, Gandhi, Aurobindo. This will supply us Indian frameworks possibly very different from each other and possibly analogous to some in other civilizations. The important thing is that we would have cognised them as Indian assumptions.

On the other hand, a meaningful understanding of Indian frameworks can only emerge through their comparison with other specific and general frameworks.

The Indian History and Culture Society intends to have a base as variegated as possible, with regard to participants, subjects to be discussed and activities to be carried out. It invites the participation and cooperation of all scholars sympathetic to these aims and ideals.

1. Approaches to Indian History

How has Indian history been viewed so far? From the imperialist or nationalist and parochical stand-point, i.e., in terms of narrow foreign or native self-interest; Communalist or Marxist, i.e., in terms of religious or economic factors; dynastic or Ethnic-oriented, i.e., in terms of political or linguistic domination; Insular, through neglect or regions, even of movements; Romantic or Cynical, i.e., oblivious either of dark or bright aspects of a given situation, and so forth.

There is need for a scientific, as well as indivisible, approach to history which would treat facts with respect and not use them to serve causes; which, moreover, would take into account all the urges of man and all the forces that fashion history, social, political, economic, aesthetic, religious, moral, etc. This should be found possible if there is : (1) amplitude of source material; (2) right discernment and impartiality in their selection, and (3) a keen analysis leading to a causal relationship of the facts. The resultant product may be termed 'Scientific History', the pursuit of which is the basic aim of this Society.

2. The Problem of Identification

(a) We need to know the past in order to find our identity. The resultant rootedness has the potential of universality necessary for an objective view of history. *We should first create and use Indian frame(s) of reference on the basis of facts of Indian history.*

It has so far been common, in fact fashionable, to use comparative and alien framework(s) which has done a great deal of harm to Indian History-writing. Indeed the various frames will coincide in their interpretation of facts up to a point but beyond that they would diverge in proportion to the difference in their underlying assumptions. It must also be noted that there is a prime necessity to possess the tool of language of our sources in order to attain sympathy with the subject of study.

(b) Every civilisation is the result of its own specific circumstances but there are also some common features among civilisations. We have to differentiate and compare civilisations in order to arrive at their unique and uniform features, respectively.

A case study of Indian History needs to be made from this point of view by studying the interdependence of various determining factors, such as physical, social, economic, political, aesthetic, ideational, etc., by treating each in turn as the most dominant.

The various equations could then be applied to different periods of history. It may well be that different equations suit different periods, even different regions, for example, once a certain degree of political, economic and social stability has been attained, the ideational and the aesthetic factors are likely to play an important role. It may thus be fruitful to view developments during the Gupta times or Early Mughal History, for example, from this stand-point and see how much did these factors effect the political, economic and social situation.

(c) In studying the uniform forces at the base of civilisations the following may be borne in mind:

(i) Independent response of different peoples to determining factors, (ii) influence through diffusion, and (iii) each civilisation's response to such influences.

3. Classification of Periods (Periodisation) & Classification of Regions

Indian historiography has seen various illogical classifications with regard to periods and regions.

Emphatic on diversities and lukewarm on compositeness of Indian culture, British writers gave the categories, North and South India which we continue to foster. They also compartmentalised Indian history into three periods and devised the inconsistent and historically incorrect nomenclature, Hindu, Muslim and British for that purpose. Since then we have renamed the periods as Ancient, Medieval, and Modern after the European model. The terms, once again are (alien) value-laden in their connotation. The whole question needs re-examination. Neither period nor region should be regarded as fixed categories. Their classification could be determined by factors, such as the nature of historical enquiry, methodological criteria, a dominant historical situation, etc. (An attempt in this direction was made by Marxist historians or by the Bhartiya Vidya Bhawan while giving titiles to each of their ten volumes of consideration the distinction between Past, i.e., Tradition, and History and the importance of the former in the Indian context.

4. Conflict and Consensus

The urges, both for conflict and consensus, are present in human beings. We need to examine the place of each as the motivating factor in individual action and societal progression.

The spirit of consensus requires concession as far as possible; that of conflict, resistance as far as possible. Progress, *status quo* and stagnation in society would depend on whether or not consensus is supported by conflict and *vice versa*, in right spirit, right measure and at right time. Thus, only a continuing watchful structuring of relationships between father and son, king and people, teacher and student would lead to, at the same time, respect for and equality with each other. Here the validity or otherwise of individual dissent (Gautama Buddha) in a general framework of stability may also be considered. We need to examine, at what time, in which fields, Indian society preferred conflict or consensus. Also whether Indian society preferred the framework of consensus within which to favour conflict or *vice versa*.

Preference for activity or equilibrium are determined by physical factors, including geography, ideational factors, i.e., pre-meditated response to physical factors, the structure of society, economic necessities, nature of political authority, etc. To give an example of the latter most: the reaction to the phenomenon of activity and equilibrium of business-class-dominated political authority would be differernt from that of intellectual-class dominated political authority.

The divergent pulls in Indian society, thus the country's size and physical features, ethnic, linguistic, religious, and cultural factors, etc., as well as the convergent pulls, natural and deliberate, may be taken into account in an attempt to discover the reasons behind the motivating factors for conflict or for consensus.

5. Ancient Terms and Modern Connotations

The connotation of terms, specially of those with conceptual content often alter radically with passage of time. The phenomenon is explicable in terms of the changing historical situation. The confusion becomes worse confounded when the terms are translated in foreign language. Apart from the problems of language and culture-differntiation, the deliberate prejudices, if any, of the translation further vitiate the situation.

The interpretation of age old Indian concepts and institutions, and thus of Indian history in general, has suffered greatly on this account in the last hundred years or so. It is imperative that we try to understand the meaning of such terms in the context of their time and place, with the help of original sources. In fact, we should try to give up inadequate English equivalents in order to get a true feel of the meaning of such terms which only comes from using them. Some such terms are : Dharma, Daṇḍa, Rāshtra, Sāmanta, etc.

6. Polity

(i) Interpretations of Kautilya polity:

(a) Social

(b) Political

(c) Economic

(ii) State versus Society

(iii) Relation between legislative, executive and judicial functions, the inner dynamics of the legistlative function.

(iv) The concept and practice of empire:

(a) Chakravarti and the maṇḍala theory, and

(b) Balance between centralisation and regional autonomy.

New Delhi
Nov. 1978

Devahuti
Prof. of History, Delhi University
(General Secretary)

Battle for the Past

D.P. Singhal

THE historian without his facts is rootless and futile; the facts without their historian are dead and meaningless. . . . (History) is a continuous process of interaction between the historian and his facts, an unending dialogue between the present and the past.

— E.H. Carr, *What is History,* p. 24.

In recent years, a number of publications of uneven quality have come out on Indian history. The writers include a wide variety of historians, professional or politically committed, and pseudo-historians, journalists or courtiers, expressing their respective attitudes and approaches. While many of these narratives are works of history, some, not unexpectedly, are inspired by nationalistic feelings, aiming at emphasising the evils of the colonial past and the virtues of the pre-colonial era; or by ideological commitment, subordinating intellectual freedom to political objectives and denouncing India's cultural past as a hindrance to economic advancement; or by communalist beliefs, looking at history in terms of religious tensions and conflicts.

In Britain, too, a great deal of historical activity relating to India has emerged, concentrating on what was regarded as the good record of the British colonial rule; or taking a nostalgic look at the "brightest jewel in the imperial crown;" or even defending the imperialist rule in toto by characterising it as a harbinger of modernisation.

Ideologically committed or inspired scholars seek to reinterpret India's past, aiming not so much at unfolding and explaining happenings in history as at employing the past to support change in the course of history. People derive immense pride and courage from the knowledge of the great deeds of their past and achievements of their ancestors. Consequently, the major battle for the past begins between those who overrate the importance and value of their historical inheritance and those who underrate or deride it. Both are trading in half-truths. However, these patriotic and ideological attitudes are important as they provide the inspiration for writing history, but to accept them as the sole or even dominating motive force in re-writing Indian history would be misleading.

The need for re-writing history arises from a variety of reasons and new interpretations are not necessarily tendentious. For example, if an Indian historian criticises a British historian, or a non-Marxist disagrees with a Marxist or pseudo-Marxist, why should it be a difference between two nationalities or two ideologies, and not a dispute between two historians?

It is true that sometimes it is not possible to separate the historicity of the historian from his ideological commitment, or his individual eccentricity from his group-consciousness. For, an historian is as much a political man as he is a professional being.

Yet history has been sufficiently used as an effective instrument of "brain washing" to deserve periodic accusations of partisanship. Historians who are seduced from truth and who stoop to distorting facts for a certain end do not necessarily assert what is absolutely false. As all questions in politics are questions of comparison and degree and in every human transaction there is a mixture of good and evil, it is possible to make a saint appear a tyrant or *vice versa* by assembling half-truths dexterously and applying searching scepticism to the evidence on one side, and credulity to the other.

Historical investigation is an unending process. Historians hardly ever agree on interpretation, but they generally admit the need for each generation to re-write history. Yet every historian claims to be telling the truth, as no one else has done before, and points out the errors of inconsistencies, of omissions, and of assumptions, in the writings to his predecessors. This can only be explained—if national or ideological bias is not involved—by realising that history is not the re-enactment of the past, but a recollection of it. The involvement of the element of human perception in recording events and interpreting them makes historical narratives, even when based on the same data, so varied. Hence, a discovery of new material, a change in outlook, values or society brought about by a revolution or advancement of knowledge, must lead to re-writing of history. Indian history is no exception. The changing concepts of history alone require periodic revisions. History is not what it was a few centuries ago; it certainly has travelled a long way from the scrupulous cataloguing of events to the tracing of their casual links.

History, therefore, is what historians make of it and claims to complete objectivity must remain untenable, as Lord Acton's hope that histories of such impartiality can be written, that can be accepted as satisfactory by every possible reader, whatever his race or creed. Even Marxist historians, who claim that history can be a science and deny the importance of the subjective role of the historian, admit that there is an element of truth in the relativity of the study of history to the historian. History is subjective, however, only to the extent that it carries the stamp of its writer's personality. As long as the story is allowed to unfold itself naturally, without any deliberate distortion or suppression of facts, it is historically an objective account, irrespective of the conclusions drawn. Once the narrative is geared to an objective, or personal bias is replaced by group-prejudice, it is at once reduced to propaganda. Writing history, therefore, is a task requiring high moral standards, as well as high intellectual capabilities. An academic historian must, to the best of his capacity, sink into and absorb the past by acquiring all the knowledge possible for the particular period or topic or region he is studying. He must neglect nothing and remain keenly aware of the gaps that remain. His task is one of selection and comprehension—selecting from an incomplete but vast mass of static records, the dynamic and living reality that once was life and then forming from that selection an account of the past that is at once both less and more significant than the past itself. Since history deals with living and changing human beings, the hardest task of the historian is to recognise and signalize every change as it comes. Small wonder Oscar Wilde said, "Anybody can make history; only a great man can write it".

The ancient period of India, with all its wealth of rich literary sources, is conspicuous for its lack of historical texts. Ancient Indian did not produce a Thucydides, but there is considerable evidence to suggest that every important Hindu court, maintained archives and geneologies of its rulers. And Kalhana's *Rājtaranginị*, written in twelfth century Kashmir, is a remarkable piece of historical literature. Despite his lapses into myths and legends, Kalhana had an unbiased approach to historical facts and history writing. He held that a true historian, while recounting the events of the past, must discard love (*rāga*) and hatred (dveṣa). Indeed, his well-developed concept of history and the technique of historical investigation have given rise to some speculation that there existed at the time a powerful tradition of historiography in which Kalhana must have received his training.

The Muslim rulers during the medieval period had a keener sense of history, but it did not stretch much beyond giving an account of royal courts, households, military campaigns and religious activities. The history of Hindu society and its culture was generally neglected. A clear chronology of the major political events is certainly established, but little is known of the changing patterns of society. It was not until the expansion of Western knowledge in India that there emerged historians who, trained in scientific techniques of historical investigation, began to explore their own past.

It was, however, the British who first began to investigate the heritage of India and who laid the foundations of Indian history. The first comprehensive history of India, *History of British India (1818)*, was attempted by the utilitarian thinker James Mill who naturally assumed the superioroity of the British over India and its past. Highly selective in his evidence, he declared that the people of Europe, even during the feudal ages, were greatly superior to the Hindus, and denied that India had reached a high degree of civilisation during the ancient period, even though the work of Sir William Jones and other European scholars had by then unearthed a volume of evidence to the contrary. Having indicated Indian society, he advocated the use of power and law to revolutionize it.

Despite the European discovery of India's past greatness and well-developed civilisation, the British, having become the paramount power in India, remained generally convinced of their own superiority over Indians, and continued to feed themselves on Mill and Macaulay, who held Indians and their literature in low esteem and sought to create "black Englishmen" in India. Even Edmund Burke's philosophical conservatism asserting the supremacy of Indian traditions and his criticism of the British "drain" of Indian wealth made no lasting impression on the British mind. They insisted on accepting the degenerate conditions of the eighteenth century India as its normal condition, looked upon their rule as part of the perennial struggle between West and East, between liberty and despotism, and characterised it as "the march of civilisation", in which authoritarianism and political power were employed to dethrone "oriental despotism" to ensure the growth of civilised communities. Seeley declared that nothing as great was ever done by Englishmen as the conquest of India, which was "not in the ordinary sense a conquest at all", and which he put on at par "with the Greek conquest of the East" pointing out that the British who had a "higher and more vigorous civilisation than the native races" founded the Indian Empire "...partly out of a philanthropic desire to put an end to enormous evils" of the "robber-states of India". Even before such a moral basis had been given to British rule in India and the doctrines a guardianship or of trusteeship had evolved, popular historians such as Macaulay and Malleson had sought to explain the British ascendancy in terms of the superiority of British individual or national character. Either the remarkable qualities of people like Clive and Hastings or the inherent virtues of the British race were held responsible for British triumphs. A Western scholar, Bearce, observed in a recent study:

"Only prejudice and rather shallow thinking could have led men to suppose that they were superior to their fellow men, that military success had enduring value, and that Britain could rule India better than Indians"*(From G.D.Bearce, British Attitudes Towards India, p.301).*

Not all British historians reacted favourably to Mill. Elphinstone, in his *History of Hindu and Muhammadan India* (1839), though cautious and somewhat hesitant, took a more favourable view of Indian history. While not disagreeing with the general political approach of the British to India, Hunter, criticised Mill and attempted to present the cultural past of India more sympathetically. He did not deny

British superiority, but wanted the British rule to rest on goodwill and to change the Indian society with the cooperation of the people.

While utilitarian thought impressed the need to assert supremacy of law on the "uncultivated society" of India, and encouraged the claims to praise Britain as the creator of Indian prosperity, culminating in the writings of historians such as Seeley, the rise of Liberalism and Marxism led to the development of ideas and movements which were opposed to political subordination and economic disparity and which attributed the alarmingly increasing impoverishment of India to the British rule. Of the scholars who pointed out that India's wealth was being drained by Britain, and who initiated the study of the economic history of India in a systematic way, these are most important. They were all non-Marxists and they published their studies at about the same time. They were William Digby, who published his *Prosperous British India* in 1901; Dadabhai Naoroji who published his *Poverty and Un-British Rule in India* in 1901; and R.C.Dutt, who published volume one of his *The Economic History of India* in 1902, and volume two in 1904. This was the heyday of British imperialism.

At the same time, Hobson in his book *Imperialism* (1902), starting from the liberal standpoint, demonstrated that the motive behind the expansion of the British rule abroad was the capitalist necessity of investing surplus capital abroad.

Between 1853 and 1857, Marx wrote twenty-three articles on India, and Engels eight, exposing British rule in India. Marx took what has been recently described as a "Europe-centered" view of India's past and saw in British rule a "double mission to India", one destructive, and the other regenerating. Britain was to lay the foundations of the material progress in India on the annihilation of the traditional Indian society. He wrote in 1853:

"Indian society has no history at all, at least no known history. What we call its history, is but the history of the successive intruders who founded their empires on the passive basis of that unresisting and unchanging society. The question, therefore, is whether the English had a right to conquer India, but whether we are to prefer conquered by the Turk, by the Persian, by the Russian, to India conquered by Briton."

"England has to fulfil a double mission in India: One destructive, and the other rerating—the annihilation of old Asiatic society, and the laying of the material foundation of Western society in Asia."

"Arabs, Turks, Tartars, Moguls, who had successively overrun India, soon became Hinduised, the barbarian conquerors being, by an eternal law of history, conquer themselves by the superior civilisation of their subjects. The British were the conquerors. Superior, and therefore inaccessible to Hindu civilisation. They destroy it by breaking up the native communities, by uprooting the native industry, and levelling all that was great and elevated in the native society. The historic past their rule in India report hardly anything beyond that destruction. The women regeneration hardly transpires through a heap of ruins. Nevertheless, it has begun."

Marxist historians have carried on Marx's view of Indian history denunciation Indian cultural heritage, as well as of British imperial rule in India.

Ignoring the concepts of economic exploitation of India, British nationalist/imperialist historians, such as Valentine Chirol, Vincent Smith, Dodwell, Coupland and others, continued to write at the beginning of this century more or less in the same strain as Seeley, made abundantly clear that India was merely a geographical expression and would relapse in old state of degneration if the firm hand of the benevolent paramount power was with drawn. "Take away the British raj", said Lord Bryce, "and the idea of unity will vanish like mist". The unifying influence of Hindu culture was not even considered. National India was generally ignored or heavily underestimated. At best, the Indian national movement was an agitation on the part of some disgruntled elite, including lawyers and the professional people, who sought high administative positions and political power for themselves. It implied that the British Government was protecting the interests of the Indian masses against the elitist and self-seeking Indian nationalists. Vincent Smith in his famous and widely read *Oxford History of India* did not mention the Indian National Congress and its demands even though the Congress had become by then a major factor in Indian politics. He thought autocracy as the normal form of governism in India and did not mention republicanism as it was known to ancient India. Verney Levett in his *Cambridge History of India* made distinction between crime and revolutionary national agitation. When Indian nation could no longer be ignored, it was described as the sole product of European liberalism, British policy and English education. Those British writers who took a sympathetic attitude towards India were run down as wicked "radicals" or "sentimentalists" who hampered the "good work of ruling India."

This attitude continued even after Indian Independence. India was thrown in British lap in a state of absent-mindedness: the British had given India unity, order and modernisation and the declining, even decadent, Indian civilisation was superseded by a superior culture. Percival Spear's *India–A Modern History,* is a fine example of this. It must be pointedout, however, that the style of a modern Smith had to be remodelled and made agreeable to suit the changed Indo-British political relationship. Today it is not possible for a writer, who desires to be listened to, to speak as frankly and boldly as Smith could fifty years ago, or Seeley could ninety years ago, or as some other imperialist historians before him. Spear's book, as that of Seeley, reflects scholarship but not an understanding of India and gives a distorted picture of the Indian people and their heritage. Unlike Seeley, he does not expound that the British acquired India out of a philanthropic desire to put an end to the enormous evils of the "robber-states of India", although he stresses clearly the anarchy prevalent at the time, and while unlike James Mill, he is not contemptuous of Hindu India, he still depicts Hinduism as containing superstitions and evil institutions. More subtly than Smith, Dodwell and Coupland, he implies that the British conquest was beneficial for the Indians, and whatever good they have today is the outcome of its impact on their society.

India, as the British found it in the eighteenth century, was in a state of utter degeneration, but it was certainly not its permanent condition. Indian civilization has a long, continuous and glorious ancestry and, all historians now agree, even at its earliest known period, it gave evidence of maturity, vitality and tolerance. It was a healthy society inhabited by a virile and vigorous people, who while "accepting joys and burdens of life, were ever searching for the ultimate and the universal." Their contributions in the spheres of art, language, philosophy, and science were remarkable and they bequeathed to humanity the *Upanishads,* the Buddha and the system of decimal notation. Their political and social institutions were very advanced for their time and they were famous for their republics, hospitals and universities. Their metaphysics and mathematics and medical science had considerably influenced contemporary civilisations and attracted world-wide attention. But Spear dilutes the effect of this vitality by making only brief and casual reference to such themes. In contrast, he gives a fresh lease to the old distorted image of India by referring repeatedly and at considerable length to features such as racial diversity, territorial disunity, rigid religious rituals and decadent social institutions.

It was inevitable that reaction against such partisan historiography should set in, especially during the period of national consciousness. New ideas and movements were increasingly captivating the Indian mind and Indians, scholars and others alike, had found new courage to defend themselves agaist undeserved onslaughts which until recently they had been content to ignore. Intense emotions of national pride produced at times equally extreme views whose historicity, however, was somewhat tenuous. They upheld the supremacy of their own culture and civilisation and tried to belittle the Western contribution. Hinduism was defended in its entirety, and certain of its ardent advocates even asserted its supremacy over other religions. Social abuses, such as the caste system were either denied or diluted or rationalised. Even *Sati* was in some ways glorified. The Britsish regime was denounced as rooted in tyranny and exploitation; their military successes were attributed either to treachery, forgery or bribery. Whatever be the verdict on the historicity of such writings, many of them were based upon sound historical research and had given a new impetus to Indian scholars to scientifically investigate their own past for themselves. Writers, such as Dadabhai Naoroji, R. Dutt, Major Basu, Savarkar, Tilak and others, can thus be justifiably regarded as forerunners of modern Indian historiography.

As a reaction against the Indian nationalism which emphasised democracy and pride in the culture of the past, which in turn meant to some people the majority rule of the Hindus, and the dominance of Hindu culture, there developed Muslim communalism. To give itself political cohesion, it emphasised the importance of religion and mutual antagonisms between Hinduism and Islam. I.H.Qureshi, a noted historian and a Musliim League leader, is an excellent example of this school of thought. He was an ardent advocate of Muslim separatism. Putting his ideas in an historical perspective, in his *The Muslim Community of the Indo-Pakistani Sub-Continent (610-1947) : An Historical Analysis* (The Hague, 1962), he unfolded the story of Indian Muslims in terms of religious conflict. Islam spread into India, he maintained, through persuasion, not coercion, and because of its supremacy over Hinduism. British domination of India was brought about by the meek submission of the Hindus, and misdeeds of the unorthodox Muslim sects, such as Shias and Ismailis (who were generally Indian nationalists), and by Akbar who practised a policy of religious toleration. These underscored the importance of economic disparities which was the main theme of the nationalists and Marxists. While disagreeing with the Marxists on the economic interpretation of the British rule, they agreed with them in their opposition to Hindu culture. The Muslim League, which embodied Muslim communalism, was founded by Muslim Nawab, but it made use of the strength of the Muslim masses.

The "Drain Theory" propounded by Burke and extended by Digby, Naoroji and Dutt (Dutt was the first Indian historian to point out that India's real problem was land and agriculture) was reinforced by theories of imperialism formulated by Hobson, influenced by Liberalism and later by Lenin under Marxist ideas. While Marxist ideas inspired Indian political workers and their influence was felt in Indian political life, they emerged rather late in Indian historical writings. There was no concerted effort by Inidan historians to interpret Indian history in Marxist terms. M.N.Roy, in his *India: its Transition* (1922), attempeted to give a Marxist interpretation of the Indian national movement. However, it is somewhat surprising that at the time of writing his book, Roy was not familiar with Marx's articles on India written seventy years ago for the New York Tribune. Roy disputed Lenin's thesis that India was going through a feudal system and asserted that India had already entered the capitalist arena. Yet, he argued, India was not a capitalist country, though it was advancing towards capitalism. It still had some elements of a feudal system which were rapidly disappearing. The nationalist movement as led by Mahatma Gandhi expressed the aspirations of the "distrustful" bourgeois. He believed that rationalism had dissolved the religious mode of thought elsewhere and it would do likewise in India. Hence he was critical of Indian tradition and culture. His work, though an important political view point in retrospect, did not seem to have made much impact at the time. Laski could write in 1927 that "the effort to read the problem of India in the set terms of Marxism is rather an exercise in ingenuity than a serious intellectual contribution to socialist advance" (H. Laski *Communism*, 1927, p. 194). It was not until 1940 that a serious Marxist history was produced by an Anglo-Indian leader of the British Communist movement. This study, *India Today*, by R. Palme Dutt, remains even today the most authoritative and reliable Marxist interpretation of Indian history. (In 1926/27, Palme Dutt had published *Modern India*, denouncing to Indian bourgeoisie as counter-revolutionary and calling for the formation of a new nation wide movement). Shortly after his work, W.C.Smith published an excellent Marxist interpretation of

Muslim communalism entitled *Modern Islam in India: A Social Analysis* (1943). Describing the transformation of the traditional Muslim community into a modern society during the British period, Smith showed that economic disparity between the Hindus and the Muslims, rigidity in Hindu social behaviour, and British policy of divide and rule were as important contributing factors to Muslim separatism as was its Islamic content. This study was banned by the British Government in India.

While there are a number of fragmentary studies, in the form of historical articles and journalistic pieces, there has been really only one study, which has come out since Indian independence, which can be regarded as a substantial Marxist interpretation of Indian history from the earliest times to the rise of British power in India. It is D.D.Kosambi's *An Introduction to the Study of Indian History* (1956). Incidentally, Kosambi was not a professional historian; he was an eminent mathematician. Despite his intense devotion to Marxism, Kosambi regarded Marx's observations about Indian economic history as "misleading", and challenged his statement that "Indian society had no history at all...". There are other studies of lesser importance. Of these, a notable one is A.R.Desai's *Social Background of Indian Nationalism* (1948), which was originally submitted as a Ph.D. thesis for the Bombay University. Another is S.A.Dange's *India from Primitive Communism to Slavery* (1948). Dange is an active Communist leader who does not recognize that Indian history does not neatly fit into Marxist periodisation, which is essential for Marxist interpretation.

Where the Marxist, imperialist and communalist historians converge is in their attitude towards Hindu culture which forms the bulk of India's heritage. Marxists, as did Marx himself, regard culture as bourgeois and anti-revolutionary. (Mao's China, where traditional culture and Confucius have been systematically demolished, is a classic example of this.) Culture, therefore, had to be denounced, including religion, God and morals, as an obstacle to proletarian change. Culture in the Indian context meant mainly Hindu religion and heritage. Imperial historians, who reacted against the "drain theory" and appeared appalled at the suggestion of economic exploitation, preferred to interpret the British rule as a missionary activity, characterising it as a march of superior civilisation over an inferior one. Hindu culture had, therefore, to be derided and held as the cause of India's predicament. Attention had to be diverted from economic exploitation to cultural contribution. The communanlists, who openly believed in religious distinctions and were naturally convinced of their own cultural superiority over that of the others, looked upon Hindu culture with disfavour. While the Marxists denounce in unmistakeable terms imperial rule and imperialist historians, they join hands with them to demolish nationalist historians, whose nationalism carried with it pride in their cultural past, and objective historians who did not seek to employ, as did the Marxist, history as an istrument of change. Marxist attacks on culture also aim at hitting at the roots and source of inspiration of nationalism, which in fact is the movement they dread most and which has effectively challenged the advance of communism in the countries of southern Asia.

While nationalism was still young in Asia, communism had entered the political arena as a third contestant, almost immediately after the Russian Revolution. Often it took with nationalist forces, partly out of its evident anti-colonial character, but mainly to exploit the powerful urge for freedom for its own ideological benefits. At times, it even cooperated with colonial or communal forces, if Party considerations so demanded; for instance, with the British Government and the Muslim League during 1940s. Asian nationalism was to be the vehicle of communism, for it was Lenin's opinion that the victory of communism in the West could be speeded up by nationalist revolutions in the territories which were then dependent on the European powers. He therefore suggested that the communist movements should unite with the nationalist movements for independence in their respective countries. Later, Stalin elaborated this theory further, but considered the nationalist movements more as revolutions in their own right, and therefore required that the nationalist revolutions should be brought under communist control and then be converted into "democratic" revolutions led by communist parties. It was during this phase that communism clashed with nationalism for the first time and since then, despite intermittent cooperation between the two, nationalism has retained its distinct personality, at times with considerable difficulty. Communist parties all over the world were asked first to fan the feelings of nationalism and then to form united fronts, the leadership of which they were required to control. The relationship between nationalism and communism remained precarious and sensitive. Communism at times mastered the nationalist upsurge, but could never fully absorb it.

Because of their constant, often clumsy, efforts to capture national leadership and their ready willingness to sacrifice national interests for extra-territorial loyalties, the communist forces repelled for more people than they attracted. They highlighted, no doubt, the problems of political as well economic inequalities, but their fanatical belief in their doctrine led them to display a callous disregard for the wishes and aspirations of the people. They soon lost the sympathy and support of the people in southern Asia which they had managed to acquire in the initial stages. In the early twenties, they were quite powerful in Indonesia, but under the direction of International Communism they embarked on a policy of adventure, which resulted in their banishment from the main political scene for many years. Of the south-east Asian countries, only in Vietnam were they able to master the nationalist upsurge and assume the leadership of national revolution. They tried very hard in Burma and in Malaya; and they succeeded in plunging these countries into a tremendous internal struggle, almost into a state of civil war. Their challenge failed mainly because they tried to disrupt and discredit the national forces in their struggle for leadership of the masses. As long as communism worked in cooperation with nationalism it flourished, but once the clash occurred, its fate was more or less sealed, for nationalism is the more powerful force of the two. Consequently, communist strategy has changed in India yet again. It is not to challenge nationalism from the outside, but to master it subtly by cooperation and infiltration democratic resistance. A period of indecision was followed by division among the Communists. They even gave way to the supremacy of nationlist urge as illustrated by their stand on Tibet. The changed political strategy inevitably conditioned *the Marxist historians, who by their very commitment to Marxist ideology, belive in employing history to change the course of history. However, it is not always possible to distinguish Marxist political writings from their historical writings.*

During the post-war period, especially since the Hungarian Revolution in 1956, there has been a tremendous proliferation of Marxism in Indian universities. Indian intellectuals also were drawn to Marxism because it appeared to be a fashionable creed, as compared with Gandhism, which was the only other alternative available and which appeared to be traditional and somewhat unmodern. The upsurge after the Hungarian Revolution was aided by the liberation of Marxist thought from Bolshevik orthodoxy and Stalinist rigidity. In the case of India, the emergence of China also strengthened belief in Marxist ideology. As a result, a large number of English-educated Indian teachers and students were attracted to the new image of Marxism and the political activity is encouraged. The new converts visualized a new image of Marxism and the political activity is encouraged. The new converts visualized a new Marxist academic tradition which was different from that of classical Marxist and which did not carry in the Indian mind the stigma of the 1942 betrayal. At the same time, the sympathetic attitude of the Government of India, first under Nehru and then under Mrs. Gandhi, towards Marxism and the Soviet Union, together with the expansion in university education, greatly enlarged the scope of Marxism for exerting influence. Once politics were brought into education, the world of history was also affected. Consequently, many historians became highly politicized. Some of them saw in Marxism a genuine way towards progress and others saw in Marxist-grouping possibilities of further success. The appointment of a

Marxist professor led to further appointments and for those young historians who sought positions in universities, the profession of Marxism became a necessary tool for self-advancement. Thus with Marxism there developed what may be regarded as Marxist factionalism. A number of writings in the form of journalistic pieces and political articles began to appear as works of history. Political power and patronage was exercised by the placing of Marxists, whether open or disguised; but always reliable, in positions of academic importance; and their works were published, translated and prescribed in universities and schools. Strictly speaking, these works are not history, though they pass as such. Some of these pieces, however, are inspiring contributions, especially those which have been written by economists or economic historians. Substantial works of historical writing from a Marxist point of view are indeed very few, excluding special studies dealing with selected aspects of Indian history.

There is much in the Marxist view of history which is thought-inspiring; economic and technological changes do determine the course of history, and class-interests do lead to class conflicts. But the sweeping generalisations and patterns which the Marxist historians draw, such as that all history has been a history of struggles between dominated and dominating classes at various stages of social development, and that history is nothing but the activity of man in pursuit of his own ends, and their manipulation of historical facts to fit into preconceived notions is distortion of history.While Marx visualised the force of economic factors in history, he did not realise the significance of cultural tradition and individual liberty culminating in nationalism and democracy. *There are no laws in history and there is no scientific exactitude in historical development. History depends on innumerable factors, many of which are unpredictable and imponderable. Historical inevitability is a myth.*

Marxist analysis of history is a worthy intellectual exercise, but Marxist penetration of the world of history is political jingoism, unworthy of academic dignity, justice and feedom.

Marxist factionalism has become so overpowering and dominant in some Indian universities that to try to present a different point of view would be to risk charges of cultural chauvinism, and anti-proletarianism. While Marxist factionalist conspiracy is permitted, the assertion of historical objectivity is not. This phenomenon is not only true of India, but of some other countries. In U.K. recently a study was conducted under the leadership of Professor Julius Gould, which finds that British universities and polytechnics had been infiltrated by Marxists dedicated to indoctrinating students and over-whelming the liberal and pluralist values of academic life. (*The Times, November 14, 1977*). This report has naturally given rise to an academic debate. Academics who are worried about the advent of a Marxist approach to subjects feel that it involves intellectually dishonest techniques. Others regard Marxism as an intellectual stimulant and a fertile system of thinking, which has been probably the most exciting intellectual development of the 20th century.

While Marxism, insisting, like religion, on the rigidity of interpretation of historical development according to the preconceived notions of society, fertilised the non-Marxist historian thought which admitted it as yet another mode of thinking, it sterilized Marxist historians who refused to think beyond the prescribed framework. Like the Church in the Middle Ages, it has sought to use history, thereby obstructing the free flow of historical development. **Since Marxist historians aim at changing history, not writing it, it is not suprising that in India, today they are rather agitating to see certain text books compulsorily retained in schools, in order thus to capture young minds, than conducting research and raising historical controversy to a higher educational level where it can properly be thrashed out, rejected or accepted. Indoctrination of students appears to be more important to Marxist historians than advancement of knowledge.**

Freedom to engage in Marxist thinking cannot be

allowed to suppress freedom of thought itself, especially in India, where thought has been more free than in any other society or culture . No true history can emerge from intellectual slavery, and as Nehru said to Khrushchev in 1959, "You do not change the course of history by turning the faces of portraits on the walls" (*Courtesy New York Post*).

New Delhi
1978

D.P. Singhal
Professor of History
University of Queensland, Australia

Saffronization vs. Distortion Through Documents

S.K. Gupta*

THE on-going debate on the need to rescue the history of the country from being the handmaid of comparative and alien frameworks touched recently 'a new high' when some historians having lost the 'battle' at home tried to raise the issue at the international fora; first at the XIX International Congress of Historical Sciences at Oslo in August 2000, and later at the XXXVI Intenational Conference of Asian and North African Studies (ICANAS) at Montreal in September–October 2000[1]. For long, these historians have been dishing out to one and all India's past on "the Left platter". While doing so, they themselves questioned some of the archetypal constructs, grand narratives or myths and notions formed and fashioned by the colonial and Euro-centric historians. However, when their own Procrustean device to map the reality came under fire, they cried foul and raised all kinds of wild allegations against a certain group of historians, the government, the VHP, the RSS and the BJP and charged them all for saffronizing Indian history.

They never cared to properly understnad the word saffron or saffronization of *kesar, kesri, kesriya* or *kesriyakaran*, and imputed meanings and import, which smack of their being pseudo-secularists or communal in their tone and tenor. As per the *Webster's Seventh New Collegiate Dictionary,* the word saffron stands both for the plant *Crocus sativus* and the moderate orange to orange-yellow substance obtained from its flower.[2] The Hindi dictionary too explains that the word *kesar* (saffron) represents a particular colour, as also *sinh* or lion. Metaphorically, the word *kesari* has been used, on one side, as the symbol of *virag* and *tyag* or sacrifice, and on the other, as of *virta and excellence* or *utkrishtta.* The meaning of the word kesariya-bānā has been mentioned in the *Allied Chambers Transliterated Hindi – Hindi-English Dictionary,* as "donning of saffron robes (for a sacrifice.)"[3] Even in case of its *kesari dhvaj,* RSS too uses the word in the sense of sacrifice. It is equally pertinent to note that at one time, the Indian National Congress had also decided to adopt saffron flag as the national flag; tricolor was a later innovation. Here too, the colour saffron represents sacrifice, wheareas white and green respectively symbolize peace and prosperity.

In fact, to give the word saffron or saffronization any other meaning would be unhistorical and full of motivations of all kinds. If motivations were not to be given precedence over the historicity of the word and its meaning, then to me, 'saffronization' of the Indian

*Former Professor of History and now Vice-Chancellor, Himachal University, Shimla.

history would mean:

i) To rid Indian history of the distortions that have crept willynilly or been injected into its skeleton, arteries and veins, or knitted deliberately, purposely and even mischievously with a design in its making or writing.

ii) To work out a methodology or a framework, which is not different from the one accepted by the historians universally, but is helpful in reconstructing Indian past with the ambience of an insider, and steers it clear of the alien sensibility, biases and prejudices.

iii) To cherish the unique and the right in our heritage, in our sense of history, as also to accept what is reprehensible, or what we need to feel ashamed of – both would deserve our attention as historians.

iv) To ensure that the former—the unique, the rich and the glorious—is neither sacrificed at the altar of willful amnesia as has happened in the past, both at the hands of foreign and Indian historians, nor it is allowed to be meshed and messed up in the Marxist 'double standards' and rhetoric of romanticisation of the Indian past.

v) To permit no one to put a magnifying glass on exceptions and accidents, and even on defects and deficiencies, or Indian frailties and infirmities so as to appear them as colossal and the Indian civilization as barbarous and primitve.

vi) To take cognizance of the spirit of an age, and reconstruct in its true colours what our forefathers lived and experienced. And not perceive the subject only in the context of modern notion of history, *kalaganana,* nation, development and progress. Or, in the context of any godfathers' lingo, i.e. in terms of the blueprints provided by Western, Christian, Islamic and social civilizations. Their importance and peripheral utility in their own right and context may not be denied but these would not be allowed to be made the be-all and end-all of historical writings on India.

II

Those historians, who purposely impute motives to any attempt at rewriting of history in the above vein and term it as 'communalisation,' 'Hindutavisation,' 'glorification,' 'indigenism' or 'indigenisation' and even 'falsification,' of India's past[4], have themselves a very poor record to unveil even if one take into consideration their efforts at documentation. Some of their works provide only a perverse kind of understanding of reality. And such a reality, on one hand, portrays the glorious, the romantic and the palatable past of their party, and on the other, tends to black out or sacrifice their reprehensible and shameful past in an exercise of willful amnesia or deliberate and surreptitiously malevolent motivations.

To provide you a test check, it may be pointed out that it is this kind of reality—either whitewashed, roseate, or blackened—that seems to surround certain parts of the ICHR volumes on *Towards Freedom: Documents on the Movement for Independence in India, 1943–44* edited by Partha Sarathi Gupta. Since it is a preliminary exercise, it would be difficult to pinpoint all the distortions or prevarications. As such it is intended to focus attention of the readers only on the documents selected and organized around the themes and focal points as contained in chapter V of the prestigious work. This chapter is captioned: "Role of the Communist Party of India," and consists of 151 documents.[5] If one glances through these documets and also takes note of the others available in the sources the editor claims to have consulted, it would reveal that well-accepted norms of editing have been largely disregarded. Why and with what purpose the documents have been arranged, organized and classified thematically ignoring the well-accepted chronological and sequential norm, i.e. placing together all types of sources of a particular date, considered to be more apposite in such kind of editing involving varied sources—neither the "Editor's Introduction," nor "General Editor's Preface." which is a rather even handed and balanced analysis of the political developments, provides any clear answer; chapter-wise chronological arrangement is not of much help in finding out as to how far a particular source has been fully and properly utilized. Even if it is accepted that the distinguished editor and historian acted in 'good faith' in arranging the documents by topics, instead fo arranging them in strict chronological order, and that the freedom he enjoyed in shaping his volumes as a genuine exercise in erudition and scholarship, the thematic scheme and constructs fail to demonstrate that the historian's craft was fairly at play. Such a suspicion increases all the more, as the volumes contain neither any subject index, nor an index of persons, with or without biographical notes.[6]

In the absence of any index, and arrangement in strictly chronological order of the documents drawn from such diverse sources as newspapers party organs, official correspondence, secret and confidential reports of the colonial administrative apparatus at the centre and spread in different provinces, papers of the political parties, persons belonging to wide variety of groups and strata, etc., it becomes still more difficult and cumbersome to mirror the political and social reality, and map the changing contours and lineaments. Not only this, it remains equally inexplicable why some kind of documents alone have received special weight, whereas others have been left out. In certain respects, the process of selection and editing has merely been reduced to editing out. Objectivity, the hallmark of a historian's craft, which strictly advocates against any *a priori* hidden agenda or against 'suppressing the truth and suggesting the false' has willy-nilly become the main casualty. It appears that ideological and political predilection has impaired the process of editing, which has resulted here and there even in an insidious form of deception. It may be difficult to spell out the precise nature of this deception unless we come to details. Here, at best an anecdote associated with the appointment of an archivist in East Friesland in 1729 may be narrated as referred to by G.P. Gooch in his work: *History and Historians in the Nineteenth Century*. It is said that immediately after his appointment, his employers informed the archivist that "after learning the secrets of our house he must carry them[the manuscripts] to the grave and reveal them to nobody."[7] He should act as the defender of the glory and dignity of the employer. Needless to mention that most of the researchers would tend to rely on these documents as authentic record of the period without ever suspecting that going to the original source would open up for them any hidden or new treasure of facts. This may be truer in case of scholars working on the Indian national movement in distant lands and countries.

The inclusion or exclusion of documents in this chapter reflects that editing has been largely done to 'write history to a purpose' and to present the roseate and to whitewash the shameful. One-seventh of the documents deal with 'A.R.P.' and reflect how keen were the members of the Communist Party of India to penetrate into the volunteer crops of civil defence so as to render service to the people during war or bombing operations. About one-tenth of the documents have been so far selected as to project Kayyur comrades as heroes. Source material obtained from newspapers pertains to only four party organs: *People's War, Janayuddha, Janasakti,* and *Daily Worker* (London); one 'letter to editor' has been incorporated from *Statesma* on 'Kayyur Brothers' and two news items from *The Hindu* about Gandhi's release and about resolving the political deadlock. It is also not clear whether the articles selected out of *Janayuddha* and *Janasakti* as available in some of the government files and incorporated in the volumes are a translation from the vernacular to English;[8] of the nine party organs, only one, i.e. *People's War* is in English, whereas others are in vernacular languages, viz. *Lokyuddha* (Hindi, Marathi and Gujarati, *Quami Jang* (Urdu), *Janayuddha* (Bengali), *Prajasakti* (Telagu), *Janasakti* (Tamil), *Deshabhimani* (Malayam), *Jange Azadi* (Gurumukhi), and *Mutiyuddha* (Oriya).[9] Similarly, nearly one-eighth of the documents pertain to 'official noting' on objectionable articles in these newspapers or on banning of the other kind of communist literature, propagandist in general, or meant for circulation amongst the party members. It is not understandable as to why some reports on the party's deeds and doings from other papers have not been incorporated. Gilbert J. Garraghan in his work: *A Guide to Historical Method* says, "Political speeches, especially those of the 'campaign' variety, the aim of which is the discomfiture of opponents, are notorious for reckless liberties with truth."[10] Some other documents included in the chapter deal with food situation, rationing, increasing strength of the communists in the trade unions, kisan sabhas, their penetration into public utility and essential services, including tramways or transport in general. Some statements are devoted to the 'fifth column'. The 'Communist Survey (July–October 1943)" records:

> July passed uneventfully with the rank and file struggling dutifully to master the intricacies of the "left nationalist deviation" and in the latter half of the month the party propagandists lent all their energies towards preventing a recrudescence of the "Quit India" disorders which they were convinced had been planned by their rivals the Congress Social Party, Revolutionary Socialist Party, Forward Block and the Trotskyists whom they brand 'fifth column"...
> Undeterred by opposition, the communists continued their counter propaganda and chose the Congress Social Party for special condemnation as "Tojo's advance guard".[11]

Whereas there is an attempt in certain documents to blacken the reality of the so-called 'fifth column', there also appears to be a strong desire to ensure that the image of certain groups does not get soiled even if the editor had to put at stake the norms of fair editing. To be precise, it may be pointed out that the above quotation is from document no. 56. If this document available in *Towards Freedom: Documents on the Movement for Independence in India, 1943–44*, pt. 2, pp. 1609–11 is minutely examined, it would reveal that there is no numbering on the paragraph or section captioned "Relations with the 'Fifth Column'" with which the document begins. This would give an impression to the reader that this is the first paragraph of the document, whereas it is actually the second.[12] Out of a total of 14 paragraphs, only 4 have been included. Why the other 10 paragraphs of the document have been edited out raises very many questions having a strong bearing on the integrity, textual fidelity and utility of the document for a researcher. The first paragraph of the document has been edited out because it does not go probably well with the 'purpose' of the editor. It certainly does not help the Communist Party of India in its image building. Instead, the critique provided in the paragraph about the functioning of the party, its claims, its strength, and the creditworthiness of its slogans, etc. rather tends to lower it. The paragraph reads:

> "...The general public has, however, remained undismayed and as indifferent as ever to communist political theories; although occasionally the practical efforts of local committees to relieve scarcity have aroused mild and generally shortlived interest. P.C. Joshi has described the Party aptly enough as 'an island in a sea of demoralised patriots' but it is becoming clear that, in the prevailing political atmosphere of frustration, his own followers are in no better heart than the orthodox nationalist. Symptoms of mallalise in the communist body are discernible..."[13]

Similarly, had paragraph 3 dealing with railway labour been included, it would have highlighted only the "humiliating defeat... [of] the party at the hands of the Royists, whom it professes to despise".[14] Paragraphs 4 to 6 pertain to their precarious position in the All India Kisan Sabha.

> "...The communist members of the [Central] Council were primed with instructions to 'win over' the General Secretary, Swami Sahajanand, who in a letter to P.C. Joshi dated July 12th had expressed his resentment at the claim of "People's War" that three lakhs of kisans "stood behind" the "pro-war" policy whereas, he affirmed, thousands of Kisan Sabha members had never even heard of the Communist Party of India..."[15]

> "...Early in September he [Shajanand] took up the cudgels again by announcing that the Sabha differed with the Communist Party of India in respect of the

"People's war" theory, the self-determination issue, support to Coalition Ministries and the communists' misuse of the term 'fifth column' to describe 'honest Congressmen' and peaceful satyagrahis."[16]

Paragraph deals with the Central Committee meeting. "...The principal speakers, P.C. Joshi and Dr. Adhikari, admitted that the Party's politcal programme and its practical attempts to deal with the food situation had evoked but a poor response from the public, and that the Party had not yet emerged victorious from its campaign against the 'fifth column' led by the Congress Socialist Party...."[17] Paragraph 9 deals with students and points out that "... Meanwhile the studnets' movement remains in the doldrums and in the more active provinces communist supremacy is threatened by rival federations. In Madras and Bomaby these have appeared under the guise of 'nationlist' organisations which profess to be non-party and non-communal but are clearly close to Congress and very hostile to the Communist Party of India..."[18] Paragraph 10 is captioned "Propaganda", and paragraphs 11–12 "Relations With Muslim League."[19]

The excerpts given above reveal two things. One, the document has been edited even as per the guidelines postulated in "General Editor's Preface" where it is emphasized: "While the editors have enjoyed considerable freedom in shaping their volumes, one common aim of the series has been to avoid an exclusive preoccupation with "high politics" and they have attempted to present, within the limits set by sources, documents relating to the activities, attitudes and ideas of the diverse classes and sections of Indian society".[20] Obviously, the paragraphs edited out do not deal with 'high politics'. What it means has not been discussed anywhere, but the dictionary meaning of the word 'high' if it is of any aid in providing an explanation, indicated that the word stands for elite, or 'extreme in religious or politcal opinion'.

It is not eqully clear as to what yardstick the editor has adopted while selecting one communist- survey, out of the two or more available in the source consulted. He has incorporated the "Communist-Survey: July-October, 1943" wheareas left out the "Communist-Survey: April–June, 1943."[21] To make my point further clear, it may be pointed out that from the historical point of view, the latter survey is even more imortant than the one included. It reads: "The quarter under review is of special interest in the history of the Communist Party of India. ...The 'All-India Congress' of the Communists held in Bombay from May 23rd to June 1st was the first in history of Party. A Party 'Congress' is the supreme authority in the constitution of the C.P.I. and its duties are to examine the work of the Central Committee, to review the statutes and programme of the Party, to lay down its 'tactical line' in respect of current politics, and to elect a Central Committee and General Secretary."[22] Besides the Bombay convention and deliberations, the document deals with such issues as Comintern dissolution, political resolutions, future plan of campaign, relations with Congress, pro-war propaganda, kisan following, labour, etc. Maybe, the editor did not think it proper to make it a part of the volume because it also records that: "the most remarkable feature of the 'preamble' to the new constitution is the ommission of any refernce to the notorious 'Draft Platform of Action'."[23] Or maybe, because the document points out that the CPI despite the dissolution of Comintern have continued to seek guidance from Russia. "Whatever may be its deeper implications, the inclusion of Stalin's name at least signifies that the CPI will continue to look to Russia for guidance. This belief is borne out by the following passage from the Convention's greetings resolution to foreign communist parties:-

" 'Greetings above all to the glorious Communist Party of the Soviet Union and to Comrade Stalin, leader of us all. We Shall win; our cause is just and there is Stalin to guide us'."[24]

A number of other documents having probably a similar ring too appear to have been edited out. For example, the letter dated 19th December 1943 from P.C. Joshi, Central Headquarters, Communist Party of India, 190B, Khatwadi Main Raod, Bombay-4 to

Iyengar, Additional Secretary, Home Department, which reads as follows has been left out:

"...We could not forego the right to expose the political and technical plans of the F.C. [Fifth Column]. We in fact consider it our bounden duty to get our people see the policy and activities of Bose and the Congress Socialist Party as being treacherous and not patriotic. We regret that in the present unfortunate political conditions, ours is the only patriotic organisation that is doing it with vigour... ."

"Thousands of middle-class radio-owners listen to the Jap Radio. My article gives them no more information than what they already know but it seeks to give them a political interpretation that Bose and his masters are not out to liberate but enslave us."

So is the case with some similar Official Notings. To cite an example, official noting of R. Tottenham dated 24.3.43 on P.C. Joshi's communications as detailed below may be mentioned. The documents addressed by or to P.C. Joshi constitute an important record of the Party and these communications have received special attention of the government and have policy implications.

"1. I have read Mr. Joshi's main letter and some of the Provincial reports. They are of enormous length...

2. From a brief survey, it would appear that most of the Provincial reports are in the same strain..

3. On the other hand, it may be true that a certain number of genuine communists have been unnecessarily, or even maliciously, arrested by the Police and it would do no harm to send the reports round to the Provinces. The fact, however, is that the communists are the sort of people who must always be "anti" something rather than "pro" anything (except, perhaps, themselves and a shadowy entity called "the people"). It would be something if we could at least drive them into the position of proclaiming themselves openly as "anti-C.S.P. and Forward Bloc" - or, in other words, "anti-left wing Congress".

4. It is interesting to note that the CPI have established personal contact with Chief Secretaries or Advisors in most Provinces."[25]

What is the most distressing part of the editing is that certain documents which were highlighted nearly a decade and a half earlier by Arun Shourie in his four articles that appeared in *The Illustrated Weekly* between March-April 1985[26] and in his book *'The Only Fatherland': Communists, 'Quit India' and the Soviet Union*[27] (e.g. see document on p. 61), neither find any mention nor scrutiny. This makes the publication still more questionable and unreliable as a compendium of research documents produced by a premier institution of India, the Indian Council of Historical Research. That the sources gain in value the more these can be shown to be reliable both substance and details, needs to be hardly overemphasized. And, however hard we might try to push these distortions and deceptions under the carpet, these would continue to cast a shadow on the functioning of ICHR. In this context, a recent article: "*Itihas-Vikriti ka Marxvadi Kuchakkar*", by Devendra Swaroop[28] is noteworthy. He pointed out that the genesis of ICHR was rooted in the fear of Ram Manohar Lohia that the documents on *Transfer of Power* edited by Mansergh and Lumby would perpetuate a myth that the British left India on their own, and that the freedom struggle and the sacrifices of the Indian people were inconsequential unless an institution was established by the Government to write an objective past of India. It is ironical that the two volumes edited by the first General Chief Editor, Dr.P.N. Chopra pertaining to the years 1937–38, one of which was printed in 1985 as *Towards Freedom 1937-47*, vol. I, *Experiments with Provincial Autonomy (1January-31 December 1937)*[29] were withdrawn from the market, whereas the other is still gathering dust in the corner of some almirah of ICHR. What was the reason for such a drastic step and to be so uncharitable to the distinguished scholar is better known to those who have controlled ICHR for long. Not only this, some of the documents, P.N. Chopra was directed to withdraw by the then Chairman before allowing the volume to go for publication. One of these documents pertained to Nathu Ram Godse's involvement in Bhaganagar Satyagraha against the Nizam of Hyderabad. In fact, since the establishment of ICHR, it has been felt by a wide variety of scholars that many of those who had been at the helm of affairs and indulged in such kind of uncharitable acts wished to fashion and fabricate Indian past to a purpose. As far back as in 1979, K.S. Lal in one of his articles on "The Role of National Bodies", pointed out that "the government of India has established the Indian Council of Historical Research makes some people think that research sponsored by it may be value-loaded if not openly propagandist".[30] To be precise, by then it had become clear that ICHR tends to use funds to give left orientation and direction to historical research in India. Writing genuine Left history *ipso facto* may not be completely undesirable. What worried him then, however, was the "Unfortunately there are many Left historians in India but little Left history". In this context, he quoted John A Garraty: "This Left history needless to say, is extremely controversial...it is one-sided and deliberately partisan...They [its authors] search not for absolute truth but for what they call a usable past".[31] K.S. Lal himself too observed that "If the Left history is not deliberately used exclusively as an instrument of propaganda for an ideology, it is surely a desideratum".[32] These observations in certain respects are true in case of *Towards Freedom* documents as well. To sum up, it won't be wrong to say that the editor used neither his pen nor scissors, nor his brush to paint, or in the words of Othello, "Speak of me as I am; nothing extenuate, /Nor set down aught in malice".[33] The purpose for which the ICHR was established seems to have largely defeated in as much as the version of Indian historical reality that the above documents provide is, as great a falsification, if not more, as the one fashioned and fabricated by a group of British historians led by Mansergh and Lumby. The only difference is that assumptions and motivations or the ideological praxis at work differ.

References

1. See abstract presented at the Round Table—Monday 28 August, 2-3:30 pm, Room 406-B, Palais de Congres, 201 Viger ouest (metro Place d'armes) entitled: "The Rewriting of Indian History: Intellectual Freedom and Contemporary Politics in South Asia," speakers listed are K.N. Panikkar, JNU, India, Chairman, Archieves on Contemporary History, India; Prof. Dolores Chew, Marianopolis College & Concordia University, Montreal; Moderator: Keith Meadowcroft, History Department, Concordia University, Montreal.

   The abstract states, "Earlier this year, two volumes of documents from the independence movement against British colonial rule - part of a mega project entitled "Towards Freedom"- submitted to Oxford Uniervsity Press were arbitrarily withdrawn by the Indian Council of Historical Research (ICHR). Box contains a statement by Irfan Habib, historian: "How these persons can have the presumption to censor the work of historians of the status of K.N. Panikkar, defies imagination. Only the Nazis in Germany over sixty years ago could have been capable of such presumption".

   It is a well-known fact that after coming to power last year the present Indian government led by the Hindu funadmentalist party, the BJP (Bhartiya Janta Party) has started an assault on all democratic and secular institutions. It has placed its members and sympathisers on the Board of the ICHR. The BJP policy on education has involved a major doctoring of school texts ruled by the BJP and there has also been a systematic and continuous attack on secular historiography, on democratic and cultural expression and minorities".

   [In this context, also see the record of Left Government in Bengal as available in Arun Shourie's book for this Government, these very historians have a great sympathy and support.

   My paper provides a critique to the volume edited by Partha Sarathi Gupta.

2. *Webster's Seventh New Collegiate Dictionary*, Masssachusetts, G & C. Merriam Co. and Scientific Book Agency, Calcutta, 1969, pp. 758, 198.

3. *Allied Chambers Transliterated Hindi—Hindi-English Dictionary*, New Delhi, Allied Chambers (India) Ltd., 1995, pp. 303, 619

4. S.K., Gupta, *The Prejudiced Past - Rewriting Indian History: Some Reflections on Concept*, New Dlhi, Indus, 1998, pp. 20-25 Cf. the criticism made by left-historians of the term 'golden age' or golden period used in the context of India with its use by Eric Hobsbawn in his work The short Twentieth Century, 1914-1991 with regard to Europe.

5. The term 'indigenism' too has been used by the left scholars in a manner so as to justify their own stance and ideology rather than to put the record straight. According to these scholars, 'indigenism' mythologises history, and only alien frameworks can provide an objective understanding of the Indian past. See India Living with Modernity by Javeed Alam.

6. S.K. Gupta, *op. it.*

7. Partha Sarathi Gupta, (ed.) *Towards Freedom: Documents on the Movement for Independence in India*, 1943-44, pt. 2, Delhi, Oxford University Press, 1997, chap. v. pp. 1532-1720.

8. See also letter no. ICHR/CHMN/99 dated 1 February 1999 fom the Chairman of Indian Council of Historical Research, Prof. S. Settar to Prof. S.Gopal, the General Editor of the volumes: "During our meeting, we discussed about the progress made so far by the Council [ICHR] in preparing and publishing the Towards Feedom volumes. There is some amount of concern among some senior scholars, whom I believe to be objective in their evaluation and constructive in their criicism, about the volumes published so far. The volume of Professor P.S. Gupta has raised eyebrows of many, for the major body of the material is stated to have been drawn from one category of source (i.e. Intelligence Report) and published without even proper Index and other such requirements expected in a volume of this kind. Some are not happy even with the Introduction written to the volume. The next volume of Basudev Chatterjee is as impressive as that of Professor Gupta in terms of the quantity, but its quality seems to have already evoked some concern. I do not know the quality contents of the other volumes, which are in press or nearing completion...If the reviewers of these volumes were to make some adverse comments on the quality of the work, things are likely to be more complicated".

9. G.P. Gooch, *History and Historians in the Nineteenth Century*, London, Longmans, Green and Co., 1952., p.12.

10. For example, see document no. 10 containing a leading article "Why does not the A.R.P. accept patriots? Is it a club for spies or citadel of fifthcolumnists?" published on Wednesday, 13 January 1943 in Janayuddha, weekly organ of the Bengal Committee of the Communist Party, pp. 1542-44. Letter dated Bombay, 28 June 1944 from the General Secretary of the Communist Party of India to the Paper Controller, Government of India, Calcutta urging special exemption from paper control order for the publications of the CPI. Home Department File no. 302/44-Poll(I), NAI, New Delhi.

12. Gilbert J. Garraghan, *A Guide to Historical Method*, Westport, Connecticut, Greenwood Press, Publishers, 1973, p.240.

13. Partha Sarathi Gupta, *op. cit.*, p. 1609

14. See Commnist Survey: July-October, 1943; it is marked as Secret and consists of 10 single-spaced typed pages. File no. 7/23/42-Home Poll (I), New Delhi, National Archives of India, see page 1 of the document marked in typing.

15. *Ibid.*

16. *Ibid.*, pp. 2, also 3-4.

17. *Ibid.*, p.4

18. *Ibid.*, p. 5

19. *Ibid.*, pp. 5

20. *Ibid.*, p. 6 also 7.

21. *Ibid.*, pp. 7-8.

22. Sarvepalli Gopal, " General Editor's Preface," to Toward as Freedom: *Documents on the Movement for Independence in India*, 1943-44, Delhi, Oxford University Press, 1997., pt. 1, p.vii.

23. This document is also marked secret and consists of 11 single-spaced typed pages. no. File no. 7/23/42-Home Poll (I), New Delhi, National Archives of India.

24. *Ibid.*, p. 1[typed].

25. *Ibid.*, p. 3

26. *Ibid.*, p. 4.

27. File no. KW 1 to 7/15/42-Poll (I)

28. For details see issues of *The Illustrated Weekly of India* dated 18-24 March 1984; 25-31 March 1984; 1-7 April 1984; and 8-14 April 1984.

29. Arun Shourie, *'The Only Fathrland': Communists, 'Quit India' and the Soviet Union*, New Delhi, ASA Publication, 1991.

30. *Panchjanaya*, 23 August, 1997.

31. *Towards Freedom 1937-47*, Vol. I, *Experiments With Provincial Autonomy (1 January-31 December 1937)*, New Delhi, ICHR, 1985, pp. xix + 1358

32. John Correia-Afonso (ed.), *Historical Research in India*, New Delhi. Munshiram Manoharlal, 1979, p 46.

33. *Ibid.*, pp. 46-47.

34. *Ibid.*, p.47

35. Shakespeare, *Othello*, V. ii. 33

Image of North-West Indian Women in Graeco – Roman Accounts

U.P. Arora*

EVERSINCE the Graeco-Roman World became aware of India, it began to take keen interest in Indian affairs. The Graeco-Roman accounts on India deal with varieties of subjects-Geographical features, flora and fauna, customs and manners, religion and philosophy, trade and commerce - infact everything connected with India and the Indians. The interest in marvels and spicy material, idealization of the country, admiration of Indian wisdom and philosophers may be marked as the dominant elements in these writings. There had also been a tendency of seeing the Indian affairs with pre-conceived Greek notions. But on account of the paucity of historical material in Indian sources, they may be treated as the best available accounts among the literary sources of ancient Indian history, despite their drawbacks.

The development of Graeco-Roman informations on India may be divided into following main periods:

1. Early Greek Authors- Age of Achaemenian domination.
2. Hellenistic-Age Authors
   i. Accounts of Alexander's Companions
   ii. Age of Ambassadors- Megasthenes and others
3. Roman-Age Accounts: Age of Compilers

Early Greek Authors

The emergence of the Achaemenian empire in the 6th century B.C. may be stated as providing the first opportunity of interaction between India and the Greek world. But during this period, the geographical knowledge of India in Greek writings was confined to the region of Indus only, i.e., the part of India (now Pakistan) included in the Persian empire. Beyond that corner of India which Persians knew, it was thought that there was nothing towards the East but a continuous desert. India was thus considered to be situated at the Eastern end of the inhabited world.[1]

During this early phase of contacts our main source of informations on Indian affairs are the Greek authors like Skylax, Hekataios, Xenophon, Herodotos and Ktesias. But the only person among them, who was reported by Herodotos to have visited India was the Greek sailor Skylax of Karyanda, serving under the Persian emperor Dareios I. Furthermore, except Herodotos the writings of these authors are known only through the fragments preserved in the works of later authors.

From the survived Greek and Latin passages on India the woman does not appear to be a significant

*Professor and Head, Deptt. of Ancient History and Culture, M.J.P. Rohilkhand University, Bareilly-243006.

subject of interest in comparison of the other aspects of the Indian life such as, philosophers, gymnosophists, economic wealth, polity, etc. Among these early Greek authors of India only Herodotos and Ktesias who had not visited the country and knew only about the North-Western India from hearsay, may be taken into account for their informations on Indian women.

Writing on sexual behaviour of some Indian tribes, who although were not within the pale of the Achaemenian Empire, must be somewhere in North-Western India. Herodotos reports that they were cohabiting in public in the manner of cattle.[2] Similar sexual practice was reported by Ktesias among the tribe known as *Kynokephaloi* (Dog-headed) living somewhere in North-Western India. According to him they were intercoursing like dogs and their women used to take bath only once in a month, i.e., at the time of mensturation.[3]

The sexual practice as mentioned above was not something confined to Indian people in Classical writings. Similar behaviour was reported by Herodotos, among the people of Kaukasos (Caucasus)[4]; among Massynoeci living at the South East corner of the Caspian by Xenophon[5] and Apollonios Rhodios[6]; and among Etruscans by Theopompos.[7]

The reference to promiscuity in North-Western region by Herodotos is corroborated by the *Mahābhārata* which states that Bāhlīka women of Sākala in the country of Madra, danced and laughed naked and indulged in sexual intercourse in open. The various literary references to the existence of *Strírājya, Strívahan* or *Nārívişaya* in North-Western India further confirm this tradition.[8] This practice was termed as *Godharma* in ancient Indian tradition, explained as *prakāśa maithuna* (intercourse in open) by Nilakantha.[9]

Hellenistic Age: Accounts of Alexander's companions

The companions of Alexander had observed three types of marriage in North-Western India. Onesikritos reports a form of marriage in Kathaea (Katha) country of India in which the groom and bride were choosing one another themselves.[10] This form of marriage corresponds with the Gandharva Vivāha of the ancient legal texts.[11] Nearchos reports a custom in which the girl was brought before the suitors assembled and was offered to that only, who had won in wrestling, boxing, running or distinguished himself in some other manly way.[12] This reminds us the episode of Penelope's suitors in Odyseey[13] or the Svayamvara of Sītā[14] and Draupadī[15] in the Indian epic texts. Aristoboulos brings to light a peculiar form of marriage which was reported at Taxila. This was the marriage by purchase prevalent among those who by reason of poverty were unable to marry off their daughters. The accounts as preserved by Strabo runs as follows:—

"Aristoboulos makes mention of some strange and unusual customs which were prevalent at Taxila. Those who are unable from poverty to bestow their daughters in marriage, expose them for sale in the market place in the flower of their age, a crowd being assembled by sound of the shells and drums, which are also used for sounding the war note. When any person steps forward, first the back of the girl as far as the shoulders is uncovered for his examination, and then the parts in front, and if she pleases him and allows herself at the same time to be persuaded on approved terms, he marries her."[16]

So far as the Indian literary sources are concerned there are numerous references to marriage by purchase since the later Vedic age in Ancient Indian literature like *Aitareya Brāhmaṇa*[17] *Mahābhārata*[18], *Milindapañho*[19] and various Puranic and Buddhist Texts. The ancient Indian legal texts also admit the form of marriage by purchase in which the parents of a girl accept the money from the boy or boy's parents in exchange of their daughter. In the eighth forms of ancient Indian marriage, the marriage by purchase known as Āsura Vivāha was condemned along with Rākṣasa, Gandharva and Paísāca.[20]

The marriage by purchase finds mention in ancient Indian literary text, but the sale of a woman in public market and sold to the highest bidder for the purpose of marriage as described by Aristoboulos in Taxila may be seen in Herodotos work, prevalent among the Babylonians. The Babylonian Custom as narrated by Herodotos was as follows:

"Herodotus tells us that once a year in each village the girls of marriageable age were collected together into one place while the men stood round them in a circle. Then an auctioneer called each one in turn to stand up and offered her for sale, beginning with the best looking and going on to the second best as soon as the first had been sold for a good price. Marriage was the object of transaction. The rich men who wanted wives bid against each other for the prettiest girls, while the humbler folk, who had no use for good looks in a wife, were actually paid to take the ugly ones, for when the auctioneer had got through all the pretty girls he would call upon the plainest, or even perhaps a crippled one, to stand up, and then ask who was willing to take the least money to marry her- and she was knocked down to who ever accepted the smallest sum. The money came for the sale of the beauties, who in this way provided dowries for their ugly or mishapen sister. It was illegal for any one to give his daughter in mariage to the man of his choice nor could any one carry away the maiden whom he had purchased without securing bail to guarantee his intention of marrying her. In case of disagreement between man and wife the purchase money could be returned."[21]

The above custom was also recorded by Herodotus among the Eneti in Illyria.[22] While comparing with the practice prevalent in Taxila we find that in Babylon too only the poor had adopted this custom, purely for getting their daughters being legally married and safe guarding them from being prostituted. However, in Aristoboulos there is no information, as to whether or not any bail was insisted upon at Taxilā as it was at Babylon to ensure that the girls so taken were only for purposes of marriage and not for any evil designs. We are also not aware whether at Taxila as at Babylon, the better looking girls indirectly paid for the safety and future of their less beautiful sisters out of the prices the former realised in terms of their comparative beauty. Notwithstanding the practice of the herald calling out the bidders in the sale and purchase of the maidens is identical with the Babylonian custom.

This practice was also observed among the Assyrians by Strabo, though in a slightly different version.[23] It appears that the marriage by purchase was named by the ancient Indians as Āsura Vivāha after the Assyrians. The prevalence of this custom at Taxilā appears to have been the result of Mesopotamian influence. There were trade contacts between India and Babylon even in pre-historic days.[24] Furthermore the inclusion of both Babylon and the Indus region in the Achaemenian Empire could easily provide an opportunity of interaction between the two. As the sale of maidens in a public market had no precedence in India, the Taxilian custom appears to be an isolated development in the bordering region, where there were also probably even the settlements made by the Babylonian merchants.[25]

In the region around Taxilā, Aristoboulos had seen the prevalence of polygamy, which he said was common along the other Indians also.[26] The Indian sources reveal that although the polygamous marriages were not uncommon and were prevalent among all the communities in ancient India, the common man was actually monogamous and it was never encouraged.

The first definite literary evidence of the custom of Satī has reached us from the accounts of the Greeks who had come with Alexander. Aristoboulos had heard that among certain tribes wives were glad to be burned up along with their deceased husbands and that those who would not submit to it were held in disgrace.[27] On the origin of this custom in Kathaea country of India, Onesikritos had heard a story according to which as the women were frequently deserting husbands or poisoning them, the law was therefore instituted to curb this practice.[28] This story is although not corroborated by an Indian source it is in accordance with the Indian tradition of recognizing promiscuity and infidelity in the North-West.

The early ancient Indian texts like the *Vedas, Brāhmaṇas, Āraṇyakas, Upaniṣads, Aṣṭādhyāyī, Arthaśāstra, Manusmṛiti* and *Yagñavalkyasmrīlī* do not mention this custom. The immolation of Vedavati's mother in the Rāmāyaṇa[29] is a single instance in the text. The *Mahābhārata* knows Mādrī of the North-West becoming Satī voluntarily and Sairandhrī being forcibly burnt with Kīcaka. All these are just exceptional instances as we find none of the widows of the Kaurava heroes becoming Satī. [30] The *Viṣṇudharmasūtra* (1st C.A.D.) is the first legal text which mentions this custom but it does not regard it as a religious duty.[31] Likewise Bṛhaspati too refers to the custom but does not mention it as binding.[32] The *Viṣṇu Purāna, Padma Purāṇa, Bhāgavat Purāṇa* and *Brhma Purāṇa* cite instances which indicate that the institution was slowly emerging between A.D. 400 to 600 A.D.[33] The only epigraphical evidence during the period comes from the Eran pillar inscription of date 191 (A.D.510).[34] The custom though practised, was no religiously sanctioned and vehemently opposed by a strong section of the intellectuals. Many well known ladies of ancient Indian history, such as Prabhāvatīdevī (Vākāṭaka queen), Mayanalla Devī (mother of Jayasiṁha Siddharāja of Gujarat), Karpura Devī (mother of Prithvīrāja III of Ajmer) and Alhana Devi (mother of the Kalachuri Narasiṁha of Tripurī) did not practice this rite, but were greatly respected on account of devotion to their husbands.[35]

The custom of Satī was not something confined to India. It was once prevalent among different tribes of North America, Africa, Oceania, China, Japan and Korea.[36] In India it appears to have been introduced from Scythia firstly in the North-West.[37] Herodotos mentions among the Scythians a custom of slaying the wives and attendants of deceased chieftains and others high in rank or social position.[38] At the time of Alexander's invasion the custom was confined to North-West only and completely unknown in the East and so remained till late Gupta times, say the 6th C.A.D.

The companions of Alexander had noticed in North- West India that women were not left behind in wisdom from their male counterpart. Nearchos informs us that along with the Brāhmaṇas engaged in philosophy and the study of nature, their wives were also studying philosophy and leading an ascetic life.[39]

The statement of Nearchos is in accordance with the Indian evidences, which refer to several women seer philosophers, and teachers of the Vedic Śākhas. In *Bṛhadāraṇyaka Upaniṣad*, Gārgī, the daughter of Vacaknu, interrogates Yajñavalkya on the prime cause of creation and several other subjects and defends strongly her point of view.[40] Maitreyī requests her husband Yajñavalkya to teach her the highest knowledge of the Ātman. Such scholarly women were classed as *brahmavādinī*. They were eligible for the upanayana and had devoted their whole life in the study of philosophy and practising asceticism.[41]

The nuns on their part as the early Buddhist literature indicates led a life of austerities and meditation, and some of them attained that higher state where all boundaries of sex differences tend to disappear. Buddha was forced to acknowledge that women are capable of Arhatship. A large number of reference in *Therīgāthā*, the *Jātakas* and in the Pali canon itself are indicative of the higher state the nuns had attained so as to consider them capable of teaching *Dharma* to the public in large. We may, therefore, believe that at least in the field of Dharma, the concepts of equality and independence of women were theoretically acknowledged which itself was by no means a small achievement.

Hellenistic Age: Megasthenes and Others

Our main source of informations on India in the period after Alexander's companions are mainly Hellenistic ambassadors like Megasthenes, Dionysios and Daimachos, among whom only Megasthenes' fragements survive at a great length. Megasthenes may be recognised as the most influential classical writer on India. He had stayed and seen more in India than any other Greek or Roman traveller. Like the companions of Alexander he was not obliged to take his notes "On the run" *(epidrm̃maden)* and so was a more patient observer than those of others, writing on India.

A woman in Megasthenes account was said to have carried the administration of Pāṇḍya nation.[42] The women warriors were mentioned as accompanying the king like Amazonian body guards.[43] No emphasis was laid on the chastity of a woman. He reported that the wives in India prostituted themselves, unless they were compelled to be chaste.[44]

In contradiction of his predecessor Nearchos, who had reported women as equal in merit with their male counterpart, in pursuing philosophy and ascetic life, Megasthenes stated that Brāhmaṇas did not share their knowledge of philosophy with their wives for fear in the first place, that they might tell some forbidden secret to the profane if they became corrupt, and secondly, that they might desert them if they became earnest, for no person who has contempt for pleasure and toil, and likewise for life and death, is willing to be subject to another, and that the earnest men and the earnest women are such persons.[45] But in another context while speaking about the Sarmanes (Śramaṇas) Megasthenes reports that "Women as well as men study philosophy with some of them, and that the women likewise abstain from the sexual intercourse."[46] After reading all these texts we find an apparent contradiction. Nearchos affirms that the Brāhmaṇas philosophize with their wives whereas Megasthenes denies it. But Megasthenes refers to ascetic women studying philosophy with the Śramaṇas, a very special group who led a hermit life. Megasthenes' sub-division of the philosopher section of the society into Brāhmaṇas and Śramaṇas seems to be very sensible, if by Brāhamaṇas we understand non-ascetics in general and by Śramaṇas ascetics in general (including the Saṁnyāsins or those of the fourth brāhmanical order, in addition to ascetics from the Buddha, Jain and other texts).[47]

Coming to Indian sources regarding the position of women, we find the corroboration of Megasthenes on several points. The warrior women bodyguards in Megasthenes' *Indikā* may be well attested both by archaeological and literary evidence. That the Pandaean nation was governed by females is not unlikely as matriarchy prevailed in south India.[48]

In Megasthenes' description of unmarried Śarmanic women who studied philosophy, we may recognise the Brahmavādinī class of women, i.e., lifelong students of Buddhist or Jain Śramanas. They remained unmarried to carry on their studies. Most of the Buddhist nuns whose songs have been preserved in the Therīgathā were maidens in well to do families, who had renounced the world for the sake of spiritual salvation. The Jain texts refer to Jayanti, daughter of other king of Kaúsambi, who remained unmarried in order to devote herself to pursue religion and philosophy.

The women among the Brāhmaṇas could also pursue philosophy. They were not deprived of education, as reported by Megasthenes. Megasthenes' report may be true in some cases particularly in the conservative Gangetic Valley, but it cannot be generalized. His predecessor Nearchos had found at least in North-West and Punjab that Brāhmaṇa women could study philosophy and pursue an ascetic life. In Indian sources Kātyāyana in his Vārttika referred to women teachers called Upadhyāyā or Upadhyayī. The necessity of coming to this new term shows that the women teachers were in large number. Patanjali referred to a special designation for the women scholars who made a special study of Mimāmsā philosophy. In the *Mahābhārata* Draupadī was called paṇḍita and fearlessly argued with her husband on all topics.[49]

Megasthenes' statement that wives in India prostituted themselves suits more to North-Western region, but is against a generally known brilliant picture of conjugal fidelity and ideal relationship between husband and wife which have been a well-known distinguishing feature of Hindu society. From Megasthenes' observation it may be pointed out that the ideal was not unoften removed from practice. Manu too exactly echoes this statement. He said, "through their passion for men, through their mutable temper, through their natural heartlessness, they become disloyal towards their husbands, however carefully they may be guarded in this world."[50] The Jātakas also mention many cases of conjugal infidelity. These instances although do not necessarily imply any general moral lapse in society, they should prove a corrective to those who idealize conjugal faith and love in ancient India.[51]

On the marriage system of the Indians Megasthenes made a general statement that the Indians married many wives, whom they bought from their parents giving in exchange a yoke of oxen. Regarding the aim of marriage he stated that some married in order to find helpmates, while others for pleasure and to fill their houses with children.[52] In order to explain the phenomenon of having many wives among the Brāhmaṇas he writes that from many wives the number of earnest children would be greater; and since they had no slaves, it was necessary for them to provide for more service from children.[53]

Polygamy has been mentioned in the Smṛti literature and the epic heroes like Kṛṣṇa, Duryodhana, Bhīma, Arjuna and Daśaratha, had each many wives. Megasthenes special mention of the Brāhmaṇas in connection with polygamous marriage is attested by the Smṛti writers, who recommend more wives for the Brahmaṇas than those of other castes.[54] But polygamy was the ideal in ancient Indian Society. The ideal models of ancient Indian marriage are the hero Rāma and his faithful wife Sītā. One Dharma Sutra[55] definitely forbids a man to take a second wife if his first is of good character and has borne him sons. Another source[56] stated that polygamist was unfit to testify in a court of law. The Arthaśāstra[57] laid down various rules which discourage wanton polygamy, including the payment of compensation to the first wife.

Megasthenes' reference to purchase of bride in exchange of a pair of oxen is in conformity with the Ārṣa marriage custom, recognised by the authors of legal texts.[58] This statement of the Greek traveller shows the popularity of the Ārṣa form of marriage in the fourth century B.C.

As regards the age of the bride at the time of marriage, Megasthenes said that in the case of Pāṇḍyan people the women were married at the age of seven and the man lived at most forty years.[59] This early marriage was considered by Arrian as quite consistant with the fact of their short life span. He said that men who became old and died so soon, must have grown into full manhood also as much earlier as their life ended earlier.[60]

The seven years age of bride may be read in some of the Hindu texts also but the other statements like the short span of life and so attaining puberty and old age comes in the Greek tradition of narrating marvels of India which Megasthenes inherits from his predecessors.[61] The *Mahābhārata* in one passage mentioned thirty and ten or twenty one and seven as the proper ages for the bridegroom and the bride.[62] Manu prescribed that the ideal marriage was one in which the bride was one third the age of the groom - thus a man of twenty four could marry a girl of eight.[63] The tendency of lowering the age for girls as evidence by the *Sūtra* texts was probably due to an anxiety to maintain their bodily purity.[64]

Although the passages confirming Megasthenes' observation of early marriage may be read in Indian texts, it was not at all common. The most of the evidences in the *Mahābhārata* are overwhelmingly in favour of the marriage of well developed and grown up girls.[65] Sītā in the Rāmāyaṇa was fully developed at the time of her marriage.[66] It has been suggested that the rules in the *Smṛtis* about the marriage of girls at an early age applied only to the Brāhmaṇas and not to other castes.[67] This is supported by the fact that the heroines of Sanskrit dramas and fiction were apparently fully grown when they married and the actual historical examples such as that of Rajyaśrī, sister of Harṣa also support this view. The numerous inscriptions discovered give little or no indication of child marriage.[68]

Megasthenes also mentions the purchase of women for kings care. According to him the care of the king's person was entrusted to women, who were bought from their parents. He further informs us that the king was not allowed to be drunk, for a stern custom ordained that a woman who had killed the king when drunk was rewarded by becoming the wife of his successor.[69] It appears that here Megasthenes was thinking of the last queen of the Śiśunāga dynasty, [70] whose intrigue was told to him by the court informants living at Pataliputra.

The trade in women has also begun during the Hellenestic period. A Rhodian Greek Callixenus (155 B.C.) referred to the display of Indian women along with Indian dogs and Indian cattle in that ornate procession of Ptolemy Philadelphus (252-246 B.C.) which took place in Alexandria.[71] So far as the dogs are concerned India was well known for their super breed since the Achaemenian days. But the Indian women meant for export were probably of the first generation in Ptolemic Egypt. This trade of women was on both ways for Poseidonios[72] wrote that Eudoxas (2nd C.B.C.) a Greek navigator during the time of Ptolemy Euergetes had shipped singing girls while making a voyage to India round the cape.

The Sanskrit plays of Bhāsa and Kālidāsa confirm Poseidonios for they report Greek women in the services of Indian kings.[73] According to Tarn,[74] this particular traffic of Greek women can hardly be earlier back than the period of Eudoxos and Indo-Greek rule in India, for in the time of Chandragupta Maurya, as Megasthenes reported, the girls were bought from their fathers.

Roman Age Authors

The works of the Greeks and Latin authors of the Roman age on India are mainly the compilations of their predecessors. Furthermore they differ from their predecessors like Alexander's companions, Megasthenes, Daimachos, etc., that with only one doubtful exception of *Periplus of the Erythraean Sea* all wrote without having personal knowledge of the country.

There are several references to Polygamy in the works of the Roman age authors.[75] We can also cite here an interesting example in the text of Pseudo-Callisthenes,[76] which is connected with a marital custom, existing among certain group of the austere Brāhmaṇas. They lived by the shores of the ocean on Yonder side of the river Ganges, but their women lived on the other side of the Ganges towards the interior of India. The men crossed over to their wives only once in a year, i.e., in the months of July and August. After spending fourty days with their wives they recrossed the river when the wife had given birth to two children, the husband did not again cross over nor go near his wife. But if a wife proved barren, her husband crossed over to her for five years and cohabited with her. And if she did not then bear a child, he no longer went near her.

There is no evidence in ancient Indian literature to corroborate this peculiar custom.

Mention may also be made of a nuptial balm, already known to the Hellenistic author Phylarchos.[77] Philostratos[78] said that unless the people attending the wedding had besprinkled the couple with this balm, the union was not considered complete nor compatible with Aphrodite bestowing her grace upon it.

The tradition of remarking promiscuous and licentious women for the region of North-West is further reflected in the work of Bardaisan of Edessa (154-222 A.D.), a gnoistic author, who has discussed customs of different peoples in his Book of the Laws of Countries.[79] One of the sections there deals with the Bactrians, who were called Kushans, i.e., Kushanas. Since the Kushanas dominated Bactria they could as well have been referred in some sources as Bactrlians. In fact the *Res Gestae* of Ammianus Marcellius refers to the Kushanas as Bactrians. The section in question states that amongst the Bactrians, who were called Kushans, the women adorned themselves of gold and pearls and their male and female servants ministered to them more then to their husbands and they rode horses caparisoned with gold and precious stones and the women did not observe chastity but had connection with their slaves and strangers, who may come to their country. Their husbands did not blame them and they had no fear, for the Kushanas regarded their wives as mistresses.

The custom of Satī which was observed in India at first by the companions of Alexander had struck the

Greeks. During the period of Roman hegemony, Diodoros Siculus,[80] who flourished under Caesar and Augustus (to at least 21 B.C.) and made a compilation of world-history in forty books entitled *Bibliotheke* gives a moving account of this custom, when the leader of an Indian contingent had died in a battle in Iran, in 316 B.C. and both his wives were eager to immolate themselves on his funeral pyre. The Greek generals had prevented the elder wife, who was with child, and gave permission to other younger. The younger one was exultant at her victory. She mounted on the pyre and ended her life in heroic fashion. The spectators were moved, some to pity and some to exuberant praise. There were also some Greeks, who found fault with such custom as savage and inhuman.

On the origin of the Satī custom Diodoros repeated the story of Onesikritos. The story was that once upon a time, wives had been so frequent to get rid of their husbands by poison that the law had to be introduced which compelled a widow to be burnt with her dead husband.

Following Diodoros, Nikolaos of Damascus[81] (b. 64 B.C.) the court historian of Herod the Great, also reported that there was a competition among the wives of deceased for mounting on the pyre, and only the most clever among them could win. The same was repeated by Cicero (b. 106 B.C.),[82] propertius (b. 50 B.C.)[83] Seneca[84] (b. 4 B.C.), Valerius Maximus[85] (1st C.A.D.) and Aelian[86] (170-235 A.D.). Everyone said that the woman selected to become Sati took it as a great honour. Philon[87] (30 B.C.–A.D.45), the head of Jewish community in Alexandria had narrated this custom to justify the act of Abraham, who had sacrificed his son.

The general image of India and the Indians in Graeco-Roman literature was an idealized one. The land was described of unusual beauty,[88] great prosperity,[89]genial season,[90] blest in highest degree[91] and its people were mentioned as the most just, long lived, healthy, very tall, truth loving, honest, peaceful and most unfortunate on this earth.[92] It may be presumed that the image of ancient Indian women in Graeco-Roman accounts would be in cosistent with this general picture of ancient Indian society. But unfortunately the passages which we have at our disposal do not coincide with this idealized image. On the other hand the reports such as cohabitation in the manner of animals, women poisoning or deserting their husbands, wives prostituting themselves, women having connection with their slaves, sale of maidens in a public market for the purpose of marriage, child-marriage,[93] etc., present an image of promiscuous, licentious and self-willed women in ancient India.

In fact except Megasthenes all Greek and Latin authors on India furnish informations mainly on North-West India and Punjab which had brought about rapid changes in the social structure and customs of the country. On account of the conglomeration of several foreign tribes, hailing from beyond the Hindukush and Pamir ranges. The foreigners settled in North-West naturally had many strange habits not liked by the orthodox culture developed in the main land. The resulting antagonism is clearly visible in the general apathy towards the North-Westerners in Indian sources.[94] The women of the North West particularly of Bāhlīka and Madra were recognized as blemish on mankind. The various references on Madra suggest that there was no restriction there on cohabitation. The echo of such a tradition about North-Western India persisted till the time of even *Rājataranginī*[95] The difference between the orthodox Gangetic Valley and unorthodox North-Western India may also be noticed on many points when we compare the reports of Megasthenes, who was well acquainted with the Gangetic Valley, with the accounts of his predecessors, whose knowledge of India was confined to North-West and Punjab only.[96] It is, thus on account of the emphasis on the description of North-Western Women, the image of Indian women in Graeco-Roman literature appears to be not in agreement with the generally prevalent notion of ideal woman-hood in ancient Indian society.

It is to be noted that except few stray references in Megasthenes, the Graeco-Roman informations on women of ancient India was limited to the Indian land known till the peiod of Alexander only. The authors of the Roman age, although preserved the accounts of their predecessors they did not benefit themselves from their contemporary reports which were obtained as a result of increased Indo-Roman trade contacts. When Arrian stated that only Alexander had made an expedition against India, he did not consider Seleucus I, Antiochus I, the Parthians, or the Kushanas and so his *Indikā* was in no sense an account of India of his times. It is regrettable that the authors of the Roman age like Arrian, Aelian, Strabo, Plutarch, Pliny, etc., overlooked the valuable reports of their period and relied upon the accounts of their predecessors. The informations connected with India of the Roman age, as furnished in the works like *Periplus of the Erythrean Sea* and Ptolemy's *Geography* are of technical nature. The former was written as a practical guide for a sea men or the coastal survey for the use of merchants sailing from the Red Sea to India, while the latter consists of tables of place names with their so-called latitudes and longitudes.[97]

It was the custom of Satī reported from the North-West, which had greatly attracted the Roman age authors, writing on India. Diodoros's moving description of the actual practice appears to be a main factor, responsible in influencing the authors of the Roman age. It removed the image of an infidel Indian woman and created the image of faithfulness. The Indian woman was now eulogised to outdo the unfaithfulness of Roman wives. Infact wearied from the complexities and materialistic outlook of their world, many Graeco-Roman thinkers found themselves to be corroborated in Indian thought. The difference between the materialistic attitude of the Graeco-Romans and the simplicity of the Indians, was repeatedly emphasized in the works of such authors. During the Roman age, India had become well-known for the wisdom of its philosophers and many Greek philosophers like Pythagoras, Democritos and Plato were reported to have derived their knowledge from India.[98] In order to accomodate in this prevalent image of the Indians, the custom of Satī was thus used by the Graeco-Roman authors in strengthening their view of the idealization of the Indians by showing a contrast between the fidelity of the Indian women and unfaithfulness of the Roman women.

References

'F and No. refer to fragments and author's serial number respectively in F. Jacoby's *Fragmente Griechischer Historiker,* hrsg. Von. F. Jacoby I-II D, Berlin 1923-30; IIIa-IIIC, Leiden 1954-58.

1. Herodotos, III, 98. Arora, U.P. 1996, *Greeks on India,* Bareilly, 16-25.
2. Herod. III, 101.
3. Ktes., Jac. No. 688, F.45 (33).
4. Herod. I, 203.
5. Xenop., *Anabasis,* V, 4, 33.
6. Apoll. Rhod. ii, 1025.
7. Theop., Jac. No. 115, F.204 (Athen., XII, 14, p.517 D-518 B).
8. For various references see Sharma, R.S., 1956, Traces of Promiscuity in Ancient Indian Society," *Proc. of Ind. Hist. Congress,* 19th Session, Agra.
9. Karttunen, Klaus, 1989, *India in Early Greek Literature,* Helsinki, p.199.
10. Ones., Jac. No. 134, F.21 (Strabo, XV, 1, 30).
11. Manu, III, 32.
12. Nearchos., Jac. No. 133. F.23 (Strabo, XV, 1, 66); F.11 (Arr. *Ind.* 17).
13. *Odyssey,* XIX, 584 ff.
14. *Rāmāyaṇa,* II.
15. *Mbh.* I, 176-81 (Crit. edn. Poona).
16. Aristob., Jac. No. 139, F.42 (Strabo, XV, 1, 62).
17. *Ait. Br.,* V, 27.
18. *Mbh.,* XIII, 44, 6.
19. *Milindapañho,* 47.
20. *Áśvalāyana Gṛhyasūtra,* I, 6; *Gautama Dharma Sūtra,* IV, 6, 13; 1, 4, 12; *Baudhāyana Dharma Sūtra,* I, 11, 20, 1-10.
21. Herod., I, 196.

22. *Ibid.*
23. Strabo, III, 16, 20.
24. For various references see, Krttunen, K., *op. cit.*, pp. 11-15; U.P.Arora, op. cit., p.1 and 10.
25. Saletore, R.N., 1973, *Early Indian Economic History*, Bombay, 407-408.
26. Aristob., F.42 (Strabo, XV, 1, 62).
27. *Ibid.*
28. Onesik, F.21 (Strabo, XV, 1, 30).
29. *Uttarakāṇḍa*, 17, 14.
30. Agrawal A.,. 1988. 'Sati-How Old? How Indian' , *Anali*, Vol. III, 91-98.
31. *Vis.*, 25, 14.
32. Br., XXIV, 11.
33. Altekar, A.S., 1938, *Position of Women in Hindu Civilization*, Varanasi, 142 ff.
34. *Corp. Inscrip. Indicarum*, III (1981 ed.), 353.
35. De, S.K. and others(ed.), 1962 (Repr. 1975), *The Cultural Heritage of India*, Vol. II, Calcutta (Ram Krishna Mission), pp. 597-598.
36. Hastings James (ed.), *Encyclopaedia of Religion and Ethics*, VI, 847, 857.
37. Dutt, R.C., 1893, *History of Civilization in Ancient India*, Vol. III, London, p. 199.
38. Herod., IV, 72.
39. Nearch., F.23 (Strabo, XV, 1, 62).
40. *Br. Up.* 2, 6 and 3, 8.
41. Srimannarayana Murti, M., 1988, "Position and Status of Women in th Age of the Liturgical Samhitās, Brahmanas and Upanisads" in *Position and Status of Women in Ancient India*, L.K.Tripathi (ed.), Banaras Hindu University, pp. 12,-13.
42. Meg., Jac. No. 715, F.13 a (Arr. *Ind.*, IX, 1).
43. F.32 (Strabo, XV, 1, 55). Also see Ḍiod. Sic., XVII, 84, 5; where women warriors were reported to have fought gloriously against the army of Alexander.
44. F.2 (Strabo, XV, 1, 54).
45. F.33 (Strabo, XV, 1, 59).
46. F.33 (Strabo, XV, 1, 60).
47. Laddu, S.D. 1991-92 "Śramana vis-a-vis Brāhmaṇa in Early History" *Annals of the Bhandarkar Oriental Research Institute*, Amrtamahotsava, Volume, Poona, pp. 719-736.
48. Altekar, A.S., *op. cit.*, p. 220.
49. Majumdar, R.C. and Others (ed.) *Age of Imperial Unity*, Vol. II (The History and Culture of the Indian People Series) Bombay, p. 563.
50. Manu, IX, 15.
51. Majumdar, *op.cit.*, p.557.
52. F.32 (Strabo, XV, 1, 54).
53. F.33 (STRABO), XV, 1, 59).
54. Manu, III, 13.
55. *Apastamba*, II, 5, 11f.
56. Narada. I, 190.
57. Arthaśāstra, III, 2.
58. Manu, III, 29.
59. Meg., F.13 a (Arr. *Ind.*, IX, 1).
60. F. 13 a (Arr. *Ind.*, IX, 6-7).
61. Arora, U.P., *op. cit.*, p.88.
62. *Mbh.* XIII, 44, 14.
63. Manu, IX, 94
64. Majumdar, R.C., *op.cit.*, p. 561.
65. *Ibid.*, p. 560. "The cases of Kṣatriya women like Draupadi, Kuntī, Uttarā and Brāhmaṇa Devayanī as well as the continuance of the custom that consummation was a part of the marriage ceremony, may be noted in this connection".
66. *Ibid.*, p.561.
67. Kane, P.V., 1930-53, *History of Dharmaśāstra* (5 Vols.), Vol. II, Poona, p.446.
68. Basham, A.L., 1981, *The Wonder that was India* (Paperback ed.) Delhi, pp. 166-167.
69. Meg., F.32 (Strabo, XV, 1, 55).
70. Majumdar, R.C., *op.cit.*, pp. 28-31.
71. Kallix, Jac No. 627, F.2 (Athen, V, 32, 200 F, 201 B).
72. Poseid., Jac. No. 87, F.28 (Strabo, II, 4, 98).
73. Keith, A.B., 1924. *The Sanskrit Dhrama*, Oxford, p.61, n.2. In the play *Śākuntalam* of Kalidāsa, Rājā Duṣyanta is represented as attended in the chase by Yavana women with bows in their hands, and wearing garlands of wild flowers. It reminds us Megasthenes' women archers employed, in the services of Chandragupta Maurya.

74. Tarn, W.W., 1951, *Greeks in Bactria and India*, Cambridge, p.374.

75. Nikolaos Damaeskanos, Jac. No. 90, F.124 (Joann Stob *Anthol*); Diod. Sic., *Bibliot.*, XIX, 33, 1; Cicero, *Tusculan Disputations*, V, 78; Valerius Maximus, *Nine Books of Memorable Deeds and Sayings*, II, 6, 14.

76. Pseudo Callisth, III, 9 in McCrindle, 1901, *Ancient India as Described in Clasical Literature*, Westiminister, p. 181.

77. Phyllarchus, Jac. No. 81, F.35 b (Athen., I, 32, 18 DE).

78. Philost., *Apoll. Tya.* III, 1.

79. Drijvers. H.JW. 1966, *Bardaisan of Edessa*, Assen.

80. Diod. Sic., *Biblioth.*, XIX, 33, 1-4.

81. Niko Dam., Jac No. 90, F. 124 (*Stob. Anthol*, IV, 55).

82. Cicero, *Tusc. Disput.*, V, 78.

83. Prop., *The Elegies*, III, 13, 17-22.

84. Seneca, St. Jerone, *Adv. Jovinianum*, I, 44.

85. Val Max., *Nine Books of Memorable Deeds and Sayings* II, 6, 14.

86. Ael. *Varia Historia*, VI, 18.

87. Philon, *On Abraham*, 182-183.

88. Diod., Sic., *Biblioth.* II, 15.

89. Dio-Chrysostom, *Orat.*, XXXV, 18 ff.

90. Nearch., Jac. No. 133, F.23 (Strabo, XV, 1, 67).

91. Strabo, I, 2, 32; II, 5, 32.

92. There are numerous references to such virtues of the Indians. See esp., Ktes., Jac. No. 688, F. 45 (16, 30, 32); Xnophon, *Cyropaedia*, II, 4, 1-9; Nearch., F. 10b (Strabo, XV, 1, 45) and F.11 (Arr. *Ind.*, XVII,1); Onesik., Jac. No. 134, F.20 (Strabo, XV, 1, 39); Megasth., F.4 (Diod. Sic., II, 36, 40, 42), F.15 (Arr., *Ind.*, XI, 9 and XII, 5), F.32 (Strabo, XV, 1, 53-54), F.33 (Strabo, XV, 1, 59); Philost., *Vit. Apol.*, VI, 11; Dio Chrysostom., Orationes, 35.

93. See above f.n.2, 3, 16, 28, 44, 59, 69, 79.

94. For example in the *Mbh.* (8, 30, 15, 10 Crit. Edn.), the North Westerners are said to be devoid of *Dharma*. They drink alcoholic drinks, eat beaf with garlic and other impure food. They sing and dance naked and drink with women in and outside th town. The Bāhlīkas of bordering region have been mentioned as descendants of the Piśācas (*Mbh 3,* 30, 44). The Bāhlīkas are the dirt of the earth and Madra women, the dirt of their sex (*Mbh.*, 8, 30, 68 Crit.ed). The bad customs prevailing in the Northern Country (North-Western) beyond the borders of Āryāvarta is found in the Deśanirṇaya Section of the *Baudhāyana Dharma Sūtrra.* (I, 1, 2, 4, ff).

95. Sharma, R.S., *op.cit.*

96. Arora, U.P., 1991-92, "The Indika of Megasthenes-An Appraisal", *Annals of th Bhandarkar Or. Res. Institue, Amṛtamahotsava Volume*, Poona, 322-324.

97. Arora, U.P., 1991, "Classical Accounts on India- Some Observations" in *Graeco-Indica; India's Cultural contacts with the Greek World* (Ed. U.P.Arora), Delhi, pp. 97-98.

98. Arora, U.P., 1991, "Roman-Age Authors on Ancient India", *Yavanikā*, Bareilly, p. 27.

Satī-Custom and Law

Saroj Gulati*

IN a patriarchal society the exploitation of women by men existed from ancient times and continues unabated even today. The traditional Hindu Society was an unequal society. In most of the *Dharmashāstras* the disabilities are imposed on the basis of caste and sex. The social evils like *satī* and female infanticide besides the inequality in the status of women with regard to property and legal rights- are some of the characteristics of Hindu society.

The custom of *satī* or the burning of the widow on the funeral pyre of her husband is called *sahamaraṇa* or *sahagamana* or *anvārohaṇa* and the word *anumaraṇa* occurs when after her husband is cremated elsewhere, the widow is burnt with her husband's ashes or *pādukās* (sandals) or even without any momento of his if none is available. Some of the *Smṛtikāras* who do not favour the burning of a widow alive, instead suggest an ascetic life for her. The customs such as *niyoga* and widow-remarriage had served to check the practice of *satī* to some extent.

The condition and status of widow has changed substantially. In the Vedic literature one finds that a widow was not regarded as a degraded person though not welcomed either. The custom of *niyoga* and for some centuries widow-remarriage was permitted though the latter was not encouraged in all cases. The custom of *satī* which symbolises perhaps the most extreme attitude to a widow gained popularity after the Gupta period though references to it are found in the literature of earlier period as well. Some of the *Smṛtikāras* suggest two options for a widow — either to become a *satī* or to lead an ascetic life, though strictly speaking it was not always left to the widow to choose the option. If she chose to live there were severe restrictions on her, including her dress, her diet and her entertainment. A widow was to live a hard life of penance and austerity. Widowhood was considered a crime, result of sins committed in her previous birth if not the present one and as a punishment for it she was to undergo hard penances.

The *Ṛgveda* and later *Brāhmaṇas, Āraṇykas* and *Sūtras* give evidence that a widow was not to immolate herself with her husband's corpse but to be brought to the world of living. In the *Ṛgveda*[1] there is a reference to a widow lying with the corpse of her husband who is asked to rise up and enjoy the world in his company and not to mourn the dead. This would not have been possible if the widow was to be burnt along with her dead husband. In *Viṣṇu Smṛti* [2] we find if a widow observes the vow of celibacy, she castes off all the sins of her previous and present birth which are responsible for her widowhood and thus she achieves heaven. In these texts, it is made very

*Reader, Lakshmi Bai College, Delhi University, Delhi.

clear that a *satī* never suffers the pangs of widowhood and enjoys the company of her husband in the heaven as well.

From the avilable historical sources one can infer that *satī* was not common in northern India till 6th century A.D. though a few references to this ritual are found in the literature of the earlier period. In the *Mahābhārata*,[3] Mādri, the second wife of Pāṇḍu, after entrusting her two minor sons to Kuntī, her co-wife, became *satī*. The analysis of this incident forces one to think that Mādrī could have saved herself from taking such a step as mothers with infants or on family way were not to immolate themselves on the funeral pyre of their husband even where the custom of *satī* was common. Kuntīi too was prepared to have the honour of becoming a *satī* but it was Mādrī who succeeded in convincing Kunti that because she was the cause of her husband's death and his unfulfilled desire, therefore, she should go with him to the next world as well to perform her *patnīdharma* (since Pāṇḍu died while having relations with his wife Mādrī—due to the curse of a *rishi*).

The references to this custom of *satī* are found in the writings of the Greeks. Strabo[4] and Diodorus point out that it was a custom for widows to be burnt along with their husbands; but an exception was made for women with children or with family, otherwise if she did not comply with this custom she was compelled to remain a widow for the rest of her life and to take no part in sacrifices or other rites as being an impious person and always held in disgrace. It would have been very interesting if we had figures with regard to the percentage of women population and the age of the widows who became *satī* during the period when *niyoga* and widow-remarriage were losing popularity and instead the custom of *satī* was favoured.

The *Yama-Smṛti* [5] tells us that a widow either enters the fire with her husband or wears herself out by asceticism with her hair shorn. The widows were considered bad omens and thus were to be avoided on auspicious occasions. An expecting mother was to be surrounded by women whose husbands were alive or who had sons. The mothers of daughters only or widows were to be avoided. This attitude of relatives and society must have had such a psychological impact on the widow that she must have found *satī* an easier way to do away with her miseries. The *Skanda-Purāṇa* [6] refers "at the sight of a widow no success can be had in any undertaking."

Though references to the performance of *satī* are found in 7th and 8th centuries A.D., it was condemned by many as well. *Bāṇa* in his *Kādambari* [7] regards it as "utterly fruitless."*Medhatithi*, commentator of *Manu-Smṛti* does not approve the burning of widows alive. According to him this is a kind of suicide and suicide of any kind is forbidden. As late as 10th and 11th centuries A.D. the common feeling was that those widows who did not burn themselves with the corpse of their husband were unchaste. Thus, to prove their chastity and not to have such a blot widows–willingly or forced—must have accepted this kind of torture. It is stated that such *satī* have great powers. Whatever they uttered came out to be true. This was another way of popularising this custom. *Śaṅkha* and *Aṅgirasa*[8] corroborate this. According to them, a woman who becomes *satī* draws her lord from a region of torment and enjoys delight with him. There she is praised by hosts of *apsarās*. If she chose to live a miserable life with her head shorn, wearing white garments, sleeping on the floor, one meal a day that too coarse one, degraded for her widowhood awaits her which probably widows shudder to accept. There are a few examples where a widow ran away from the funeral pyre but was brought out of hiding by her own son who was afraid of being excommunicated by the society.

Polygamy also led to the custom of *satī*. There are many references to the dissatisfied queens whom kings did not visit for years. In such circumstances, men in the disguise of women were found living in the *aṅtaḥpura*.[9] After the death of the king there must have been a big question with regard to these queens who may be young and old. If a king could not keep them in check during his lifetime how could one expect them to be chaste after his death. There was every possibility of their having relations with men of lower caste as well.

There are many references in the literature of 11th and 12th cnturies indicating that widows who became *satī* never suffered the pangs of widowhood in their future births.[10] This way these *Dharma´sāstrakāras* tried to influence and encourage the widows to become *satī* especially when they were young, uneducated and economically dependent upon their husbands and confined to house-hold duties. The traditional image of the male as "protector" owes a great deal to the notion that women cannot defend themselves and men must therefore take charge of their lives. One of the causes of women's subjugation was their economic dependence on men. As long as women were denied the opportunity to earn their living there could not be equality between the two sexes. This custom was not common among the widows of lower castes, though they were not educated either but they were economically independent. They could earn their livelihood. With the demise of the husband they did not become liabilities on their relations. The rigidity of caste system also made it difficult for widows of higher castes to live a normal life. On the other hand, if a widow of lower caste was allowed to live she did not pose any threat to the rules of endogamy.

It was around 6th century A.D. that we find an indication of preference for the partition of joint family.[11] This too must have helped in popularising this custom. In a joint family, husband's family or relations could look after a widow but when alone, it must have been quite difficult to manage. Secondly, if her husband had not left any property then there were financial problems. If he had left any property but died without a son the property was to go to his wife. If a man was a member of a reunited family and if he died without a son the property was to go to his brothers and not to his wife. Thus, by eliminating the widow there was not only material gain for the family of the husband but the sanctity of religion and morals could be invoked in the process. It is further added that the brothers of the deceased shall make provision for the widow till she died and that too only then when she remained faithful to the bed of her husband.[12] This too was enough to make a widow's life hell because at any moment she could be labelled as unchaste and thus her allowance could be cut off. The circumstances and the life were made so dreadful that a widow shuddered from living such a life.

The political, besides the social and economic, conditions of early middle ages forced women to become *satī*. There are quite a few examples showing that the Rajputs, while fighting against the Turks and Afghans, could foresee their defeat either killed their wives and children themselves or if they had enough time, they sent their women, children and wealth to distant places and then faced enemies.

In the earlier period, many references are found with regard to the resentment shown by the widows against this practice of *satī*. In Kalhaṇa's *Rājataraṅgiṇi* [13] we find a queen who did not want to become *sati*, bribed the brahmanas, gave them plenty of gold from time to time, and thus saved herself and ruled her husband's kingdom. The matter does not end here. Later, she fell in love with a boy of lower cast, got members of her husband's family killed and nominated her brother's son as crownprince. This incident could have been used to deter people from favouring widow-remarriage as that was the outcome if a widow was allowed to live. A patriarchal and patrilineal society could not accept a wife's relations inheriting the throne, "a wonder of the world which had occurred in this realm."[14] This must have made the lawmakers to put forward *satī* as the only solution. These *Dharma śāstrakāras* had thought of another alternative and that was enforced widowhood. This was superior to burning of widows because that was more practicable but the inclination of *Smṛtikāras* was towards the custom of *satī* because it did not risk the morals of the group.

In the beginning it seems the custom of *satī* was prevalent among kshatriyas but later brāhmaṇas and other castes adopted it.[15] As regards shūdras, it was not recommended for them though one or two examples of *satī* are found among them as well—"Women of rank seem to have been the most willing to accompany their husband's remains to the funeral pyre. The women being members of warrior class whose men folk died freely and readily in the battle, the pyre seemed a smaller matter and sacrifice a fairer thing than to the women of peace loving races."[16] While discussing the relationship between the castes and *satī* it can be said that with regard to brāhmaṇa widows it was a very late development. In the *Vyāsa-Smṛti* [17] for the first time the custom of *satī* was recommended for brāhmaṇa widows too though another option of getting her head shaved and live austerely was also given. *Mitākṣarā* or *Yājñavalkya Smṛti*[18] adds that this duty of *anvarohaṇa* is common to the women of all castes from brāhmaṇa to the chāṇḍālas provided they do not have small children or are in the family way at the time of their husband's death.

Brāhmaṇas had a great hold in most of the northern parts of India. To attract these brāhmaṇas to their kingdom the kings started giving liberal grants to them, free of taxes. According to D.C.Sircar[19] the epigraphic references show a large number of brāhmaṇa migrations from Ganga-Yamuna Doab to Orissa and from Madhyadesh to North Bengal. The epigraphic and literary sources show that these are the places where this custom was popular. As the number of land owning brāhmaṇas increased some of them became more interested in their secular than in religious functions. The absolute and hereditary rights over the spiritual and ideological mechanism helped them in acquiring economic and administrative rights. The rise of feudalism transformed the status of shūdras from the position of slaves and hired labourers to that of agriculturists. The brāhmaṇas and kāyasthas played an important part in the administration. In such circumstances, there was danger of mixing of two castes, i.e., *varṇasamkars*. It is possible that to avoid this kind of situation the brāhmaṇa widows were asked and expected to burn themselves. Secondly, the land grants were given not only to individuals but to a group of brāhmaṇas. In the absence of a widow, the other brahmaṇas were to share the property of the dead brāhmaṇa.[20]

There was lack of mobility so far the question of artisans and peasants was concerned, whereas there were no restrictions for brāhmaṇas. Though a grantee had the right to retain or remove the tenants from the granted land, the peasant was not allowed to leave the land on his own. It was primarily because of agriculture, trade and commerce, that a large number of people from the labour class were needed. Therefore, there was remarriage of widows and absence of *satī* among them.

Apart from literary, there are epigraphic evidences to the self-immolation of widows. These records make it clear that the *satī* stones were worshipped and to encourage widows to follow the path, pandits endowed it with virtue and admired it.[21]

European travellers who came to India in 16th and 17th centuries A.D. inform that widows who were to burn on the funeral pyre of their husbands were in fact made senseless by drugs so that they may not feel the pain.[22] It can be argued that it was not so because of the pain but to avoid the screams of the widow so that no body knew how she was forced to perform this ghastly act of suicide. It is further added that sometimes they were hurried, dragged to the pyre with warnings, prayers and promises. If they hesitated they were driven forcibly to the fire and if they tried to leap out they were held down by poles and hooks. Edward Terry[23] writing in 16th century about *satī* comments that to be free from 'shame' many young women were ambitious to die with honour and thus becoming *satī*. To burn with the spouse, he adds, was voluntary and no body compelled them for this act. It is possible that was what he gathered from the relatives of that widow or people present there but what that 'poor creature' wanted or was going through nobody knows. Once a widow decided to burn herself, her relations and her own parents, most joyfully accompanied her and when the wood "is fitted for this hellish sacrifice and begin to burn, all the people assembled shout and make noise so that the screeches of the tourtured creature may not be heard."

Nicholas Worthington's (1612-1616)[24] views on *satī* are somewhat different from his contemporary observers. He is of the view that widows were not compelled to become *satī* and where they were it was by their kith and kin so that they do not bring disgrace to the family. He cites the example of girl of 10 years, whose marriage was not consummated, calmly enters the fire with the turban of her husband who died in the battlefield. (Perhaps the observer missed the drugging part, which is not done publicaly. It seems next to impossible that such a small girl was not afraid of fire and entered it quietly). Those who refused, he says, had to shave their head, break jewellery, they were not allowed to eat, drink or keep company with anybody. They led miserable lives till their death, "never any account was made of her after."

Another traveller of the 17th century refers,[25] "there are hundreds and even thousands who do not do it there is no reproach as is asserted by many who write that those who neglect it incur the reproach of their caste." Rajputs, khatrīs and baniās practiced *satī*, he continues. A travelller writing during the reign of Shahjahan, observed that the governors did not readily give permission to self immolation of widows but they could be bribed to do so. Willian Hawkins [26] who was in India in 1608 also confirms that Hindu widows burnt themselves along with their dead husband "because they will be registered in the books for famous and most modest and loving wives who, leaving all worldly affairs, content themselves to live no longer than their husbands." Thevenot [27] says that the fate of Indian wives (Hindu) is different from that of their husbands as women cannot marry a second time even when their first husband is dead. They dare not, he adds, marry again. They have their hair cut off for even though they may be five or six years old; if they do not burn themselves then they have to live in perpetual widowhood which happens very often but then they live wretchedly for they incur the contempt of their family and caste for being afraid of death. Bernier[28] narrates an incident of a child-widow from Lahore who was of 12 years and was burnt alive. He states that she was weeping bitterly as she approached the dreadful pit. She was forced by three or four brāhmaṇas, assisted by an old woman "who held her under the arm, forced the unwilling victim towards the fatal spot, seated her on the wood, tied her hands and feet, lest she should run away and in that situation the innocent creature was burnt alive.

When Willian Bentinck became Governor General in 1828, he was intolerant of this inhuman practice which was condemned not only by Britishers but by reformist group of Indians as well. He proclaimed it to be illegal and banned it in all those states, which claimed union with the Company government. The seven years of William Bentinck's rule, from 1828 to 1835, forms an epoch in the administrative and social reforms in India. The most remarkable and memorable act is the abolition of *satī*. It was he who took such a bold step. He gathered public opinion with regard to the custom of *satī*. The result of the survey was that many were in favour of its abolition and many in its contiuance. It was not only by the efforts of Britishers that the custom of *satī* was declared illegal but social reformers like Raja Ram Mohan Roy were actively opposed to this practice. Ram Mohan Roy's determination to abolish this custom became stronger when his own sister-in-law (brother's wife) was sacrificed on the altar of this custom. He gave full cooperation and support to implement the law when Bentinck carried the Regulation in Council on December 4th 1829 by which all who abetted were guilty of "culpable homicide". Regulation XVII of 1929 made the burning or burying alive of widows culpable homicide, punishable with fine or (and) imprisonment. When compulsion or the use of drugs deprived the *satī* of free will, the offence was punishable with death as murder. It came in to immediate operation in Bengal and was adopted in Madras and Bombay (Mumbai) six months later. In Bombay (Mumbai) this Legislation was adopted with some modification, that the offence was murder if the widows were 18, if not, then maximum of ten years imprisonment was prescribed. Though this law was widely welcomed yet there was resentment and opposition from a group of orthodox people who formed a committee, obtained 800 signatures and appealed to Privy Council to restore *satī*. They appealed that the law interfered with their ancient and sacred rites. It was again because of Ram Mohan Roy's efforts that this appeal was dismissed. This Regulation probably helped in lessening the number of sati but did not cease it altogether. It appears that Britisher were unable to abolish this old practice because of opposition from orthodox group of Hindu leaders. Bihar had *satī* cases in 1901, 1903, 1904 and 1905, there was one case in a small village in Punjab in 1905 and in 1906 a few cases from Kanpur and Calcutta had been reported. It had persisted even in the 20th centuy. The case of Roop Kanwar is a well-known exampple besides many reported and unreported cases. In spite of all this people still visit *satī* temples and worship *satī-sthals*. There is a satī-mela every year at Jhunjhunu, Rajasthan, the place to which Roop Kanwar belonged to. The state goverment announces three day's official holiday to enable people to people to visit that place and admire this heroic deed of *satī* who brought name, fame and prosperity to her village. (financial gain from the shops constructed around that place, sale of the photographs of smiling Roop Kanwar while entering the fire and the visitors). This was the case in 1987 when a girl of 18 years, from an affluent family fell victim of this inhuman practice. It is the incident of a recent past, which aroused public opinion against this practice that the government was forced to pass a law against this. A team of journalists visited the place to get first hand knowledge of circumstances in which she was 'murdered'. The team quoting eyewitnesses said,"Far from being voluntary, Roop Kanwar's *satī* was the result of the girl's helplessness." The team was told that when the body of Roop Kanwar's husband was brought home the preparations of *satī* began immediately. Roop got an inkling of this and tried to hide in one of the barns in the surrounding fields. She was, however, dragged from there and put on the fire. A young boy claimed to have seen her swaying as she walked to the cremation ground while another saw her frothing at the mouth[29]. It is believed that there are many reasons for thinking that such an event as a voluntary *satī* very rarely occurs: few widows would think of instinctive horror from the first hint of sharing her husband's pire, will be at length gradually brought to pronounce a reluctant consent because distracted with grief at the event without a friend to advise or protect her, she is little prepared to oppose the surrounding crowd of hungary brāhmaṇas and interested relations, either by argument or by force—"

The members of the investigating team who went to Rajasthan in 1987 reported that haste, family pressure, opium, the photographs of women imprisoned by wood and coconuts in the neck high pyre-the very notion of 'voluntary"satī becomes a mystification. It is said that some Rajputs compensate for loss of political and economic power by making *satī* a matter of identity—an identity sought to be reclaimed with unashamed cowardice by burning women. A recent study of Roop Kanwar's self-immolation indicates that if she had lived beside the usual restriction laid down for a widow such as eating very plain food or sleeping on the floor or wearing white clothese only, she would have been subjected to taunts that she was responsible for her husbands' death and been to sexual exploitation. Her parents too would have closed the doors to her. On the other hand by 'immolating herself' she had earned a place in the folklore of the area, blessed her parents and her in-laws' family for the next seven generations and in addition brought prosperity to both the families and her little village.[30]

It is reported by a district official that the warrior class, to keep its women in check while the men were away for long periods, deliberately introduced the worship of goddess *satī*. Even today, he claims, 90% of the upper castes live and work outside the village leaving their wives behind. It is also stated that with the abolition of *zamīndārī* system, the Rajputs lost a coniderable degree of economic power. This in turn forced them into the job market where unemployment has been on the increase and the competition getting stiffer and stiffer. The life of a Rajput widow is still intolerable. The Rajput women, who even now are not permitted to work on the fields, are ostracised when widowed and segregated; not allowed to participate in social gatherings and forced to wear white and "cannot even eat pan."[31]

This incidence of *satī* led Rajsthan government to promulgate the Rajasthan *satī*. Prevention Ordinance 1987, which provided punishment for instigating *satī* and for glorifying *satī*. It empowered District Collectors and District Magistrates to remove unauthorised work on *satī-sthal* and prohibit unauthorised construction of *satī* memorials. This was later replaced by a central enactment, the Commission of *satī* Prevention Act 1987. This Act received the assent of the President of India on Jan'3rd 1988 and the Act was published in the Gazette of India on Jan. 6th 1988 (Act No. 3 of 1988). This act was to provide for the more effective prevention of the commission of *satī* and its glorification and for matters connected herewith or incidental there to.

According to this Act (a) all officers of Government are hereby required and empowered to assist the police in the execution of the provision of this Act or any rule or order made there under. (b) All village officers and such other officers as may be specified by the Collector or the District Magistrate in relation to any area and the inhabitants of such area shall, if they have reason to believe or have the knowledge that *satī* is about to be or has been committed in the area shall forthwith report such fact to the nearest police station.(c) Whoever contravenes the provisions of sub-section 1 or sub-section 2 shall be punishable with imprisonment of either description for a term which may extend to two years and shall also be liable to fine. Further a person convicted of an offence under sub-section 1 of section 4 in relation to the commission of *satī* shall be disqualified from inheriting the property of the person in respect of whom such *satī* has been committed or the property of any other person which he would have been committed.

A *satī* is honoured because it is a proof of the perfect unity of body and soul, between husband and wife and of devotion beyond the grave. According to Lakshmīdhara,[32] "She who shares her husband's joys and sorrows and dies on his pyre, is the ideal of chastity." The text of this kind forced widows to take such an extreme step. Women need to be treated like human beings only. They do not want to be worshipped like goddesses after they have been sacrificed on the altar of religion. A widow should not be treated as out caste for no fault of hers. A woman who has lost her husband is miserable and the attitude of the society and relatives make it worse what the fate has ordained for her. The Commission of *satī* prevntion Act of 1987 has by all possible means tried to dissuade and abolish this inhuman custom which some people with vested interests have kept it alive in the name of religion and tradition. It is reported that the new Act on *satī* is worth appreciating as it widen the scope of abetement and provides more stringent punishment.[33] But the new laws are not the only solution. What is more important is the enforcement of this law more strictly and punishment to the culprits. It should be seen that there are no such false notions like the chastity of a woman is proved by her self-immolation. The attitude of the society needs to be changed if we want the same rights to be given to women as are given to men.

References

1. *Rig Veda, c.*18.8.
2. The Institute of Vishnu, III, ch. XXV, v. 14. Jolly Julius (Tr.), *The Sacred Books of the East*, reprint 1965
3. Mahābhārata (Adi-Parva) (Sambhava-parvan) 1, 116.25-31 (critical edition) 18, 170, Poona 1971.
4. Strabo, 62; Diodorus, XVII, 91 and XIX, 33 Macrindle, J.W.—*Ancient India as Described in Cassical Literature*, 69, 1901.
5. Yama-Smrti—Gharpure, J.R.(tr)-Smṛti-Chandrikā (Vyavahāra-kāṇḍa), pt. III, P. 531.
6. *Skanda-Purāṇa* (Kāshī-Khaṇḍa), ch. V, 71-84, p. 6 Nag Sharan Singh (ed.), 1982.
7. Bāṇabhaṭṭa, *Kādambarī*, ch. II, (*annuchheda*-177) p. 172; Vasudeva Sharan Aggarwal (tr.), 1958.
8. Śaṅkha and Aṅgīrasa — *Gharpure*, J.R.(tr)—Mitaksharā (Vyavahāra-kāṇḍa).
9. *Kathāsaritasāgara*, pt.I, L.I, T.V, vv.60-61.
10. Hemachandra—*Trishashtishalakapurusha-charitam*, Vol. V, Book VIII&IX, pp. 421-22, Johnson, H.M.(tr.)1962.

11. Sharma, R.S., *Indian Feudalism,* p.113
12. *Nārada-Smrti,* XIII, 25-26.
13. *Vyāsa-Smṛti,* ch. II, v.53 Dutt, M.N. (tr.),1908.
14. *Mitāksharā on Yājñavalkya* I,86.
15. Sircar, D.C., *Land System and Feudalism in India,* p.62 (1966)
16. *Narāda-Smṛti,* XIII, 25-26.
17. Sharma, R.S., *Perspective in Social and Economic History of Early India,* p.196, 1983, 31 pp. 309-10
18. *Rājataranginī,* T.VI, vv.317-321 Pandit, R.S. (tr.) reprint 1968.
19. *Ibid.,* v.366
20. Paithinasi-Mitākshara on *Yajñavalka-Smṛti* (Achara), 86.
21. *Epigraphia Indica,* vol. V, 1898-99, No.A.113.
22. Foster, W. (ed.), *Early Travels in India,* p.29
23. Foster, W. Supra notes 51 and 90.
24. Foster, W. 119.
25. Sen, Surendranath (ed.), *Indian Travels of Thevenot and Careri,* 119, 1949.
26. Bernier, supra note 31 at 314.
27. *Times of India* (Delhi), Oct. 4th 1987 Ed.), *Early Travels in India,* p.29.
28. Foster, W. supra note 51 at 323
29. *Decan Herald,* Oct 21st 1987
30. *Times of India,* (Delhi) Oct. 25th 1987
31. *Times of India* (Delhi) Sunday Review, Oct. 4th 1987
32. *Ḳrtyakalpataru* (Vyavahāra), p.636
33. *Indian Express* (Delhi), Oct.8th 1987.

Faqirs and Darveshs in Hyderabad during the Nizam's rule

Vandana Kaushik*

EVEN after the decline of the Mughal Empire, Mughal culture continued to flourish in many parts of the country. This is more true of the erstwhile Hyderabad State. Art, architecture, dresses, court etiquette, ornaments, food habits, languages, all carried the legacy of the Mughals, to such an extent that Hyderabad came to be known as Mughalia State.[1] The Asaf Jahi rulers of Hyderabad continued many traditions of the Mughal Emperors. One of them was providing liberal grants to the scholars, saints, religious places of worship, etc. The first Nizam was particular in distributing such grants to only worthy persons. Hence a class sustaining on charity alone and in turn contributing little to the society could not flourish. But as the power of the Nizam gradually diminished, with the increasing British interference in the internal matters of the state, and the economic conditions deteriorated due to recurring of famines, the number of indiscriminate charity grants also showed an upward rising trend. Nineteenth century Hyderabad witnessed the growth of a class, commonly known as Fakirs, Derweshs, Bairagis, Gosains, and so on. Sufi saints were also included in this class.

Nizam-ul-mulk Asaf Jah I was a religious man. He used to visit the shrines of various Sufi saints regularly and make large charities. Still, he was careful that his charities were not wasted or allotted to underserving persons. For instance, before sanctioning scholarships to the needy and poor students, the first Nizam himself used to take oral tests in Arabic and Persian grammar.[2] Mansaram, the Secretary of the Nizam, has described a specific anecdote in Masir-e-Nizami to establish his deep rooted concern for the religious men, on the one hand, and his anguish for adopting a luxurious life styles by the fakirs, on the other. The anecdote is recorded as under[3]:

"The Fakir (Darvesh) made a request to the Nizam, who was visiting the tomb (Rauza) of Shah Abdul Qader situated near the Zafar gate of the city of Aurangabad. 'There are no allowances fixed for the conduct of the festival for feeding the poor, for lighting the Rauza, etc. The Fakirs and the pilgrims visiting the tomb are put to great trouble. Many of them are addicts of tobacco and hukka. Fakirs find it very difficult to stay in the precincts of the Rauza'. In passing orders on the request of the Fakirs, the Nizam remarked, 'the Khanqah (Monastery) is a place of light (Noor). What connection can this Noor have with fire and tobacco. A man can put down his taste for tobacco by the light that is within him'. The Nizam appointed Sayyad Muhammad Magni to the custody of Rauza and gave a Sanad accordingly."

*Reader, S.P. Mukherjee College, Delhi University, Delhi.

The policy of the first Nizam prevented to a certain extent the unnecessary growth of parasite class in the society. However, the situation changed during the period of Nizam Ali Khan, his son and successor afterwards. Rulers and nobles took keen interest in several non-political activities and surrounded themselves with all kinds of religious persons. Sufi Saint Shah Kamatar who composed a Masanavi in proto-Urdu, has recorded that Nizam Ali Khan while passing through the streets of the city threw coins on both of his sides. In whatever route he went through, fakirs of that area could get enough for one year. "Some Pirzadas received so much money that those who did not even have a sack now could build havelis".[4]

Last few decades of the 18th century Hyderabad are known for the political upheaval and continuous warfare. As a result, the state was proceeding to weakness. In this period, famine occurred year after year which reduced a large chunk of the population to extreme poverty, some of which later on merged with the existing class of *fakirs*. During 1792 to 1797, Telangana region witnessed one of the worst famines. The price of essential commodities rose very high. Grain was not easily available in the markets.[5] *Jawar* was sold at the rate of 8-9 seers a rupee. In 1792 markets in Hyderabad had remained closed for three days. Poor people could not obtain anything to eat. Angry mob looted the houses of the rich merchants and had gathered in front of the palace of the Nizam. They were so much agitated that they put the Royal Palace on fire and could be dispersed only after the Nizam ordered his guards to open fire.[6] The situation was so grim that a number of people were forced to sell even their children.

The famine continued for 5 full years. Gulam Samadani has recorded in *Tazkir-e-Nirmal*, a Persian text published in 1906, that although the Nizam had passed orders to show leniency towards the public, Vankaih Pandit the Talukdar of Nirmal had exploited the situation. He not only collected the full tax during the famine of 1794 but had snatched away even their animals. The whole district of Nirmal was virtually deserted.[7] People blamed the Nizam for their miserable condition and felt greatly relieved when Nizam Ali Khan passed away in 1803.[8]

The above-described unfavourable economic conditions of the Telangana region can explain the growing number of fakirs in the city of Hyderabad during the early decades of the 19th century. The poor and unemployed could easily feed themselves as *fakirs*. The famous courtesan of Nizam Ali Khan, Maha Laqa Bai or Chanda, as she was popularly known, is well known for her charity to the *fakirs*. On various fairs, such as the Fair of Khat Darshan and Urs of Maula Ali, she used to feed thousands of *fakirs* everyday and also distributed rupee 1-5 to each one.[9] The occasions used to be so much attractive that a number of *fakirs* used to come from far off places.[10]

A contemporary traveller Sri Enugula Veeraswamy who has written *Kāśiyātrā Charita* in Telugu, also observed the presence of numerous *fakirs* in and around Hyderabad city during the early nineteenth century. He was travelling from Madras to Kasi and when he reached the Hyderabad City in 1830, he wrote, "The region from the river Krishna up to Hyderabad is full of *fakirs* and these *fakirs* praise you and ask for alms. I had to give them a few cowries."[11] In the year 1832, food grain became so expensive in Hyderabad that people openly came out on the streets and threw mud and stones on the *sawari* of Nasirud Dawlah, the IV Nizam. In the year 1833, food grain was sold at the rate of 8-9 *seers* a rupee. People were forced to resort to begging.[12]

Chandulal was the Diwan during the early decades of the nineteenth century. Most of his actions as Diwan were fully supported by the British Government at Calcutta. In turn, he also implemented the suggestions of the British government. Thus, under the leadership of Chandulal, the Nizam was reduced to a mere figurehead, as the Diwan even without caring whether the Nizam approved his actions, did everything.[13] Philip Medows Taylor, who was sent to Shorapur by the British Resident of Hyderabad, has recorded in his letter of 24th September 1843 the indiscriminate charity of Chandulal in following words:

"He was an able man in his day, there is no doubt, but he has broken within the last four years and his unscrupulous desire of money to squander away on all sorts of Gossains, Bairagis (sic) and faqirs. Whoever pretended to see a vision of heaven in which Chandulal was seated along with Hindu or Mahomedan sages and holy persons, was sure to receive large presents, or if the knave was a cleverer than usual, he got a jagir(sic) (a village) of a thousand Rupees a year settled on him for life."[14]

During this time, some cheats and thugs also took advantage of the situation and got them disguised as *fakirs*. The biography of Amir Ali Thug has provided ample details of his involement in the *thugi*, in the disguise of fakir. The number of *fakirs* increased during the reign of the fourth Nizam when the law and order situation in the city was extremely deplorable. Thieves and robbers also known as *Dagas* disguised themselves as *fakirs* and used to sit at various places from where traders and rich people used to pass. Their gangs remained hidden in the dark and bushes. Thus they were merged in the large population of *fakirs* in the city. *Tad Shah ki Baradari*, a place where Tad Shah, a *fakir* had lived, was a well-known place for the regular occurrence of *thugi* as it was situated on the 8 mile long deserted route from Hyderabad to Koh-i-Sharif.[15]

Afzal-ud-Dowlah, the V Nizam, was very generous towards *fakirs*. He gifted *jagirs* to some of them.[16] Not only these *fakirs* became rich, they had their agents too who looked after their interest. The names of some of such *fakirs* and their agents, such as Shah Kamosh, Sardar Ali Shah, Mote Shah, Habib Jilani, Shah Nur-ud-Din Qadadari, Mahboob Ali Shah, Khwaja Sahib, Mukka Shah, Chunti Shah, Chaman Ali Shah, Dolachi Shah, and Lahara Shah are recorded in *Rudad-i Hyderabad* Daccan.[17]

Nawab Sarver-ul-Mulk, was a Mughal noble. He reached Hyderabad with great difficulty after 1857. He has recorded in detail the prevalence of *fakirs* and their influence in Hyderabad, in his biography *Kaınam-i-Sarwari* in the following words:

"In those days Noor-ud-Din Shah Qadari, a resident of the Punjab was the Pir of the Deccan ruler and His Highness had so much regard for him that he used to send him baskets full of gold and jewellery."

During his reign (V Nizam), the city contained a very large number of Darveshs with strange nomenclature. For instance, 'Dungi Shah' and 'Nakki Shah' were a few peculiar names. These men led the life of ease and luxury and had their *vakils* at the palace, who in their turn, had become wealthy. But the most influential of the *Pirs* was Hazarat Nur-ud-Din Shah Kadri."[18]

During the later half of the 19th century, Salar Jung contributed substantially in transforming Hyderabad from a Medieval to a Modern city. Yet, there was one aspect which remained totally untouched, and it was the class of *fakirs*. Their number and distinct groups increased considerably. One Urdu writer Mohammed Abdul Shakur Saida has described in "Sair-i-Hyderabad" in 1904, the various groups of these *fakirs*. He writes, "There are so many *fakirs* in Hyderabad, which could rarely be found in any other city. On every nook and corner, they are to be seen in hundreds. Because a lot of charity is prevalent in the city they move in groups. They earn so much that each of them gets at least Rs. 15 to 20 per month. Every type of food is available to them. They are invited to *Dawats* (lavish parties) also. Crippled also receive enough to eat. These *fakirs* move with umbrella, with stick in their hand and blanket on the back. If it is dark, they also take lantern. Some also carry swords. Rowdies are common among them who demand money on all occasions, happily or sadly by using force. One group belongs to *Rafai fakirs*. They show some *tamashas* and ask for money by torturing their own body. In this way, they influence people to come forward to give alms to them. They have their own *Pir* also where they gather and practice their nefarious tricks. *Pahadi fakirs* also ask for alms using the same tricks."

"Gosains are now faqirs only in name. They have monthly income provided by the state and nobles. They have so much money that they also involve in money lending business. Although some of them have lakhs and crores but still they go on practicing their profession, some times with their disciples wearing heavy gold jewelry on arms, neck and waist, they move out with their followers. They accept if somebody offers voluntarily, otherwise they do not ask."[19]

The description of different groups of *fakirs* in Hyderabad by a contemporary writer at the turn of the century establishes beyond doubt that their influence in society was substantial. They also enjoyed a good status and their well being was assured. Perhaps, these factors contributed in motivating a number of persons in becoming *fakirs*. However, it does not mean that all *fakirs* were not religious persons. But it can be safely concluded that the degenerating economic condition, large number of charities and poor law and order condition prevailing during the late eighteenth and early nineteenth century Hyderabad contributed considerably towards the growth of a class which was commonly known as fakirs.

References

1. Nawab Jiwan Yar Jung Bahadur, *My life*; autobiography of Nawab Server-ul-Mulk Bahadur. London, 1932. p. 68.
2. Mansaram, *Jawabit-i-Huzur* Pur Noor. Persian Mss, Osmania University Library, Hyderabad. p.33.
3. Mansaram, *Masir-i-Nizami*. Persian Mss. p. 113 as quoted by P. Setu Madhava Rao in Eighteenth Century *Deccan*, Bombay, 1963. p. 81.
4. Shah Kamtar, *Dastan-i-Nizam Ali Khan*, ed. by Dr. Sahibjada Mir Nizamuddin Ali Khan. Hyderabad, 1978. p. 60. (In Proto-Urdu).
5. Ghulam Imam Khan, *Tarikh-i-Rashidudin Khani.*, Hyderabad, 1868. p. 304. (In Urdu).
6. Mohammad Ismail, *Jami-i Tarikh-al-Imade-Sarar Jung*. Urdu Mss. Salar Jung Museum Library, Hyderabad, p. 447-8.
7. Gulam Samadani, *Tazir-i Nirmal*. Printed Persian. Hyderabad. 1906. p. 100-1.
8. Mohammad Najmul Gani, *Tarikh-i-Riyasat-i-Deccan*, Hyderabad, 1930. pp. 402-3. (In Urdu).
9. Gulam Samadani, *Hyat-i-Maha Laqa*, Hyderabad, 1906 . p. 26. (In Persian).
10. Abdul Hai. *Mamalkat-i-Asafiya*, Karachi, 1978. p. 362. (In Urdu).
11. Enugula Veraswamy's Journal, *Kāśiyātrā Charita*, Edited and Translated by Sri Sitapati and Sri V. Purshottam from Telugu, Hyderabad, 1973. pp.25-6.
12. Kadir Khan Munshi, *Tarikh-i-Asafi*. Tr. from Persian by Dr. Zabun-nisha Begum. Hyderabad, p. 141 and 147 (Unpublished).
13. Nani Gopal Chaudhuri, *British relations with Hyderabad*, Calcutta, 1964. p. 207.
14. Cadel, Sir Patrick, ed., The Letters of Philip Medows Taylor to Henery Reeve, London 1947 p. 117–118.
15. Mir Dilawar Ali Danish, *Riyaz-i-Mukhtaria*, Printed Urdu, Hyderabad, 1942, p. 126, 148.
16. Mohammad Husain Khan, *Mahbub-ul-Salatin*, 1885. p. 444. (In Urdu).
17. *Rudad-e-Hyderabad Dakkan*, A short history of Hyderabad from 1853-63. Urdu Mss. Salar Jung Museum Library. Hist. 248. Folio No. 42-7.
18. Nawab Jiwanyar Jung, *op.cit.* p.80.
19. Mohammad Abdu Shakur Saida, *Sair-i-Hyderabad*, Hyderabad. 1904 p. 80-1. (In Urdu).

The Mahabharat for Harappa

S.P. Gupta*

NEVER before such a Mahabharat for Harappa was fought as it is fought today. It is almost a street fight between the historians and the archaeologists. The common man is bewildered since the Harappan Civilisation is as much a part of Indian History (it includes Pakistan for historical reasons) as several other civilisation, such as the Mauryan, Sungan, Gupta and many others for the knowledge of which we require archaeological sources as well as historical sources. The reason is simple. Archaeologists, of late, on the basis of recent discoveries and detailed examination of the results of previous discoveries have started realising that all that was said about the Harappans and their civilisation in 1930s, 40s and 50s may not have been all that true. For example, Sir Mortimer Wheeler had written that the city of Harappa was attacked and destroyed by the Rigvedic Aryans. He accused Indra, the Lord of devas, for this devastating attack. He also visualised a similar act of vandalism at Mohenjodaro on the basis of some scattered skeletons in the Lower Town found by Sir John Marshall. Archaeologically it has now been completely falsified; Harappa was never attacked by any one, much less the so-called Aryans. Prof. George Dales and Prof. K.A.R. Kennedy also proved beyond doubt that the so-called "Massacre of Mohenjodaro" has been a complete myth, no one ever invaded the city and no one really died in the battle field. The former published in 1964 an article entitled "The Mythical Massacre of Mohenjodaro" in *Expedition,* No.6, pp. 36–43 a journal of the Philadelphia University, U.S.A. The latter published his article entitled "Skulls, Aryans and Flowing Drains: the Interface of Archaeology and skeletal biology in the study of the Harappan Civilization" in *Harappan Civilization: A Contemporary Perspective* edited by G.L. Possehl (1982), pp.289–95. It, therefore, also shows that the theory of Aryan-Dravidian conflict in Harappa had no archaeological basis and all talks about the Aryan invasion of Indian had been floated for reasons other than sound and scientific history and archaeology.

Dr. Romila Thapar of late says that the Aryans came to India slowly and gradually from the western gateways in the second half of the 2nd millennium B.C. though such a theory of peaceful migrations was propounded earlier also. But when asked to give solid archaeological evidence for even this theory, she talked only in terms of possible 'alternative models' which is, as well all know, highly subjective. There is hardly a group of peope identifiable in archaeological records which crossed the Indus system of rivers in

*Chairman, Indian Archaeological Society, New Delhi-16.

the 2nd half of the 2nd millennium B.C. and reached the Saraswati-Drishadvati system of rivers on the banks of which lived the people who composed the hymns of the Vedas, historians call them Vedic Aryans. In my book *The Archaeology of Soviet Central Asia and the Indian Borderlands,* 1979, Vol. II, I have shown that not even one archaeological culture of Central Asian origin of this period ever crossed the Indus, including the Keltminar Culture and the Bishkent Culture often quoted in favour of Central Asian theory of Aryan homeland. After all any theory of migration of people from one place to another must be proved on archaeological grounds since people generally moved with pots and pans, items of arts and crafts as well as tools and weapons, hence archaeologically identifiable. Unfortunately, neither Prof. Shereen Ratnagar has been able to dig them nor Prof. Suraj Bhan the two camp-fallowers of Prof. Thapar.

The recent most issue of the international journal *Man and Environemnt* (Vol. XXV,No.1, 2000) puts on record the unscientific attitude of Prof. Shereen Ratnagar through several review-papers by biological and archaeological scientists like B.E. Hemphill, J.R. Luckacs, S.R. Walimbe and P.P. Joglekar, particularly when she argued agaisnt the anthropological results showing no significant foreign elements in the Harappan population as well as the continuity of that very population during the post-Harappan period. However, it does not mean that it was not the mixed population but the biological differences are of a kind which shows that in the Harappan cities villagers from distant places came and lived together. Hence marginal variations in terms of physical anthropology.

Some historians are maintaining that there was no horse at the Harappan sites and attack Raja Ram's latest theory based on a misunderstood seal-image but seal or no seal the Harappans at sites like Surkotada, Kalibangan, Mohenjodaro did use in everyday life true domesticated horse identified by Indian and Hungarian palaeo-zoologists like Dr. Bhola Nath, Dr. A.K. Sharma and Prof. S. Bokonyi. This they did by identifying the biological remains of the domesticated horse (*Equus cabalus* Linn.) in the form of actual bones as I have mentioned in my book *The Indus-Saraswati Civilization* published in 1996. It is also true that even the Vedic people used horses in their everyday life. Regrettably, a lot of noise is being created on this issue through glossy magazines apparently for reasons other than the cause of sound history and archaeology.

The Harappans invented a system of writing sometimes written from right to left and sometimes left to right. It was boustrophedon system of writing and not exclusively right to left or left to right. Those who quote B.B. Lal, they do not quote him fully and faithfully. He proved his theory in the case of a few potsherds bearing scratched inscriptions and a couple of seals from other sites but it does not mean that the Harappan script was written from right to left everywhere and in all situations. One wonders as to why so much of dust is being raised on this issue in popular journals unless it is aimed at fighting in ideological battle with some people.

Max Muller called the Vedic people as nomadic tribes, knowing nothing of the cities and city life. However, it has now been proved beyond doubt from the letter he wrote to his contemporaries (these letters have now been published) that his ultimate aim of studying the Vedas was to show their utter primitiveness so that Christianity was able to spread its wings in India; it is common knowledge that he never visited India. However, Bhagwan Singh's book *The Vedic Harappans* published in 1995 has pricked the bubble and shown to the world that the economic model built by Max Muller for the Vedic Aryans was thoroughly motivated and was inspired by Macauley, who had helped him in getting his job. The fact is that the Vedic people were fully familiar with a variety of *pucca* houses, agriculture and agricultural produce, mining and metallurgy, manufacturing of goods and trading, sea voyage and sea trade, including piracy, and above all, writing. The Harappan and Vedic convergence has more than 500 references in Vedic texts and Harappan archaeological remains, according to R.S. Bisht, the excavator of Dholavira, a major Harappan site in Gujarat. We refer to his recent-most article entitled "Harappans and the Rigveda: Points of Convergence", published in *The Dawn of Indian Civilization,* Ed. G.C. Pande, pp.393–442.

Irfan Habib talked of the Sraswati river in terms of very small stream existing in Haryana but while saying so he is suppressing the most scientific work done on this river by Remote Sensing method by India's top most scientists who have traced the dried up channels of this river in the deserts of Rajasthan. I would like the readers to refer to the article authored by Prof. Yash Pal and others in 1984 under the title "Remote Sensing of the 'lost' Saraswati River" re-published in *Frontiers of the Indus Civilization* edited by B.B. Lal and S.P. gupta. Pakistani archaeologist M.R. Mughal also supports it on the basis of his field-work published in his book entitled *Cholistan.* During the last 16 years many more works by geologists and linguists have appeared, all of which support the findings of Yash Pal *et al.* according to which the old course of the Saraswati was very vast, at places 8 to 10 km in width, as was proved by a Swedish expedition led by M. Hanna Rydh at Rangmahal in 1952–54 on the basis of borings made in the dried up bed of the Saraswati river. According to recent geological studies the Saraswati had emerged from the Himalayan glaciers which constantly fed it with water but due to tectonic movement an upheaval took place which put barrier to it depriving the river of its major source of water. Thus, it is clear that the Saraswati had emerged from the Himalayas and flowed towards Cholistan in the Bahawalpur region of present-day Pakistan. Only last year (1999) the Geological Society of India, Bangalore has brought out a more than 300 paged volume of more than 30 articles entitled *Vedic Saraswati* under its Memoir Series (No. 42) edited by B.P. Radhakrishna and S.S. Merh. One wonders why Irfan Habib chose to ignore these findings except for the fact that these may have been inconvenient to his ideological commitment. Is it really scientific history?

Some people are questioning my effort to change the prevalent nomenclature to that of the Indus-Saraswati Civilisation. This I am doing because of the present ground realities which are vastly different from that existing in 1931 when Sir John Marshall edited the volumes of the culture he named *The Indus Civilization.* Then there were not even 50 sites known to us, today the number has gone up to 1400. Then the sites were known to exist only in the basins of the Indus and its tributaries but today these are found located in the basins of the Saraswati and its tributaries. The number of sites in the valleys of the Indus sytem rivers is not even 150 while there are more than 500 sites in the valleys of the rivers of the Saraswati system. Thus, is it not a fact that this civilization was the gift of not only the Indus river but also of the Saraswati river? Thus, do these new discoveries not demand the inclusion of Saraswati in the nomenclature of this civilization? What is wrong in it? Where is the question of Saffronising Harappa? This is in fact the scientific history.

Notes, News and New Source Material

New Archaeological and Epigraphical Findings at Deorkothar

In the year 1999–2000 Dr. P.K. Mishra and his colleagues in the Archaeological Survey of India, Bhopal Circle, made a startling discovery of a stupa-complex with a piece of inscibed Mauryan pillar and remains of several inscribed railings of the Śuṅga period at a site called 'Deorkothar' (Barhat) (Lat. 81°40''E Long 24°56'N) located in Tehsil Tyonthar, Distt. Rewa in Madhaya Pradesh on National Highway No. 27 (Rewa-Allahabad), around 5 km north-west of village Katra. It was the famous Dakshiṇāpath. The complex includes four brick built stupas, thirty stone built stupas and some monastic complexes as well as water-channel system of 3rd-2nd century B.C. This hilly area has many rock shelters, some with paintings. Stupa No. 1, a burnt brick structure, rises to 9.5 m. The construction is based upon concentric circles with the hollow spaces filled with very compact clay and mud. Uprights and cross-bars as well as copings, all of local Vindhyan sandstone, have also been found. There were gateways also.

The six line Mauryan Brāhmī inscription on Aśokan pillar fragments, so far 20 of them have been found in the excavations, read as under:

भगवतो बुध ....

उतर मित्रो उतर मित्रस अ.......

भड् भड्स आतेवासिना दि नु......

उपासकस आतेवासिना वजयसव.....

धमदवेन के क डी के न बस ति ये.......

उसपितो मं भो आ आचरियेन क सि

'The inscription opens up with Lord Buddha. It pertains to the erection and dedication of a stone pillar at this place by upāsaka and his disciples in the memory of Buddha, the Englightened One. The inscription speaks about an Āchārya, named Dharmadeva, and his three disciples, Uttarmitra, Bhadra and Upāsaka, who used to reside in the monastery.'

The second stupa, Stupa No.2, located some 400 m south-west of No.1, was also built like the No.1 but its exact height is only 2.75 m and diameter 11.20m.

The inscriptions on the railings are in 2nd century B.C. Brāhmī and show their nature as didicatory. Some of them read as under:

(1) कु त ग म ते द ये दानम्

(2) तेजितये दानम्

(3) उजेनकस ध(म)

(4) क ढ़ क द

(5) स मि स...खि...त स प च

(6) क स प्र ते त ये दानम्

(7) गं ग द त र

(8) प द न म

(9) त सु

(10) ग म (र) व

(11) उदय पुते वेलये दानम्

The railing pillars bear decorations in low relief showing lotus in round, twirling lotus, lotus with drooping petals, conical lotus buds, a pūrṇaghaṭa on three tiered pedestal.

P.K. Mishra

Book Reviews

D.N. Jha, *Ancient India: In Historical Outline.* Revised and Enlarged Edition. Manohar, Publishers & Distributors. New Delhi 1998. pp.216, Price Rs. 250.00

This is the second, revised and enlarged, edition of the book *Ancient India: An Introductory Outline,* first published in 1977. For two decades it has received the attention of readers interested in the syllabus of competitive examinations. The book does not mark any departure from the commonly followed scheme of chapterisation, excepting the titles suggested by the author from his understanding of them. The eight chapters are : Introduction; From Pre-history to the Harappan Civilization; The Aryans and the Vedic Life; The material background of Religious Dissent: Jainism and Buddhism; The first territorial states; The first empire; Invasions, Trade and Culture c. 200 B.C.—A.D.300; and The myth of the Golden Age. Chapters 4 and 5 cover almost the same chronological span. Chapters 5 and 6 are concerned predominantly with political history.

The main merit of the book is its readablity, which is not burdened with heavy footnotes. This evokes the interest of the reader and sustains it throughout. The author appends descriptive bibliography for those who would like to go into the details of his formulations. It removes the charge, often levelled by readers against books on ancient India. One wonders why this type of narration, available for the history of other periods and countries, was not often attempted for ancient India.

The non-specialist reader may, however, find difficulty in distinguishing a factual statement from an opinion expressed by the author.

The functions of a historian in his craft involve the use of imagination and the drawing of inferences. This is both his duty and his prerogative. The use of rights and privileges has to be disciplined; it is not to be uncontrolled and unlimited.

The book contains many statements, which are not historical facts but opinions of the author, whose true nature a common student may not easily understand. To illustrate, we refer to a few instances: The author notes that in the *Ṛgveda* 'the cow is described in one or two places as not to be killed (*aghnyā*)[2], but refuses to accept its obvious inference and instead adds 'this may imply its economic importance' (p.46). His view about the social classification of the spoils of war was certainly the basic reason for the emergence of the fourfold division of society. But the phenomenon was also linked with the process of assimilation of the aboriginal non-Aryan people by the various sections of Aryan society (p.50). Dr. Jha notes (p.42) that the whole concept of race based on skeletal measurements and colour (of the hair, skin and eyes) is now regarded as invalid. But, at many places he uses the argument of racial difference for important statements, e.g., dispersal of Aryans (p.43) —Dasas and Dasyus (p.45)—Aryan features (p.49)—Origin of Vasistha and Agastya (p.50). He states that the wives of the gods' are called *ganas* collectively, which is reminiscent of group marriage prevalent among the Aryans at some stage' (p.52). The tendency to give a free play to imagination, without caring for facts, can be seen in the account of the vicissitudes of the Vedic assemblies acquiring an aristocratic character and the enhancement of the king's power in the later period; priests beginning 'to be subservient to rulers, so as to strike mephistophelian bargains'; and a great development in the sacrificial cult taking place 'with rising royal pretensions and priestly ambitions' (p.58). The emergence of the *gahapati* as a comparatively wealthy head of the household is taken to indicate 'the growing disparity of wealth within the society', 'common people, slaves and labourers seem to have coveted his wealth and wished him harm; often he is depicted as maintaining a bodyguard to defend himself' (p.68).

The author chooses to argue by twisting an argument. He says that 'if the establishment of Muslim rule marks the beginning of medievalism, several contemporary west Asian countries as well as Pakistan will have to be placed in the medieval age' (p.24). The argument is not that with Islam began medievalism; in the scheme of periodisation in Indian history there were many important changes in polity, society and cultural history in the medieval period, which also witnessed the coming of Muslim rulers.

Dr. Jha makes a bold assertion about the development of religions and philosophical systems in the pre-Buddha age, without referring to the historical evidence about them, when he remarks: 'The conflict between the Vedic religious practices and the aspirations of the rising social groups led to the search for new religious and philosophical ideas which would fit with the basic changes in the material life of the people' (p.69). It will be hard to believe that the statement adequately covers the search for truth which motivated Siddhartha and Mahavira. His statements involves a long drawn argument when he says that the concept of *ahimsā* helped agriculture and Buddhism was acceptable to the village-folk because it showed a greater awareness of the needs of agriculture (p.73). Some other statements, made in this connection, are equally subjective: 'The inhabitants of Magadha and Anga were held in low esteem because they traded in certain commodities'. 'Buddhism ... gave its support, indirect though it may have been, to usury'. Buddhist attitude to certain features of urban life, it is asserted, is in contrast to the Brahmanical attitude of prohibition of food prepared in shops and condemnation of prostitution (pp.74-75).

The description of a legal and judicial system as 'an important weapon of coercion in the hands of any ruling class', (p.88) though it may be applicable in many cases, is uncalled for in a text book of the present nature.

The view about the origin of the territorial republics in the sub-Himalayan region is assumptive and subjective. It is traced to 'the reaction against the pattern of life that evolved in the later Vedic period'; it 'was aimed at the abolition of the growing class and sex distinctions and directed against the acceptance of religious practices which took a heavy toll to cattle-stock' and 'against the hereditary kingship bolstered by the brahmanas, who arrogated to themselves all the rights and privileges to the exclusion of all the other sections of society' (p.89). The birth of a republican and democratic political frame-work is 'attributed to the socio-political conditions of the period. In the early period members of ruling elite obtained a portion of the booty of war and tributes collected from the vanquished. But in subsequent times, when the victorious tribal chiefs came to occupy prominent and hereditary royal positions in the territorial states, they claimed all revenues for themselves. The leading members of the tribe resented the situation, and demanded the right to collect taxes from the peasants and the right to bear arms and maintain their own army' (pp. 89-90).

One would like to know more about important statements 'the almost complete disarming of the rural population' by the Maurya government (p.101). The absence of reference causes difficulty and confusion. Here we refer to four statements based on the *Arthaśāstra* (pp.97-98). They are not located in one portion of the original text but occur in widely separated chapters. A regular student of history may also find it difficult to ferret them. I have tried to locate them; if the author means different passages, then my apologies. The rule about the transfer of land to someone else on the failure of the farmers to cultivate it (II.1.10) is not applicable to all lands but relates to newly settled areas. The statement that 'associations or groups could not be formed by members of the lower orders' possibly refers to II. 1. 32. It mentions the ascetic sects, corporation (*saṅgha*) and association with agreements (*samayānubandha*) which are not to be settled in the *janapada* (country-side). A corporation only of those born in the same place (*sajāta*) is to be settled. An association with agreement only for a joint undertaking (*sāmutthāyika*) is to be settled. The passage does not refer to associations or groups of members of the lower orders. The other passage translated by Dr. Jha as 'As for settling a land with the four castes, the one where the lowest castes predominate is the better because it will permit all sorts of exploitation' is possibly VII.11.21. Here, in the chapter dealing with the pact for unsettled land between two kings, the passage mentions the different type of benefits to accrue from settling various occupational people on that land. Of the four *varṇas* the settlement of lower *varṇas* is preferable for its capacity to yield all kinds of benefits *(sarvabhogasahatvād),* the one of farmers being preferable for plentifulness and definiteness of agriculture, that of cowherds for starting agriculture and other undertakings, and of rich traders for the benefit of stores of goods and loans. *Bhoga* here refers to enjoyment or benefit and not to exploitation. This follows from the fact that the following passage refers to the benefits of agriculture, cattle-rearing and business, the three constituents of *vārtā* (applied economics).

The author mentions a water-tax as one of the principal taxes collected by the state (pp.98-99). But the consolidated list of taxes in the *Arthaśāstra* does not include it; the omission is significant because it would have been an important source of State income. Dr. Jha possibly relies on II.224.18. This is a provision in the chapter dealing with the arrangement of cultivation on crown land by the Superintendent of Agriculture (sītādhyakṣa). It cannot be made applicable to common peasants cultivating their own land.

Dr. Jha points out that Kautilya devotes one full chapter to the methods of systematically breaking up free tribes (p.102). Here he is referring to *Artha* XI. 1. This book deals with *Sangha* (*sanghavṛtha*), which means a corporate set-up which is closely knit (*samhatva*) and here is to signify an oligarchy, if not a 'republic'. The chapter does not aim at breaking them, but at gaining them (*lābha*). Those who are friendly (*anuguṇa*) are to be won over (*bhuñjita*) with conciliation and gifts, and those hostile (*viguna*) through dissensions and force (XI.1.1-2).

The subjective opinion of the author sometimes does not respect a positive statement in the original source. He refers to Kauṭilya recommending the recruitment of Vaiśyas and Śūdras in the army but dismisses their actual enrollment as soldiers as 'extremely doubtful' (p.103). At places the force of his logic is neither clear nor convincing, as for example, when he interprets the support of the Vaiśyas to heterodox sects Buddhism and Jainism as 'an expression of their resentment against the two higher castes' or when he infers from the provision of punishment to a Śūdra who calls himself a Brāhmaṇa, steals the property of gods or is hostile to the king, that some Śūdras 'bore hostility to the priestly and ruling classes' (p.103).

Without pointing out any supporting argument or evidence, the author describes Śrī on the *Arthaśāstra* to 'have originally been a non-Aryan fertility goddess who found her way into the brahmanical religion' (p.104). Though admitting that actual instances are not recorded, he remarks that 'the ideological conflict between the Vedic brahmanas and the followers of the newly born protestant creeds may have been a potential source of social and religious tension' (p.105).

In analysing the causes of the disintegration of the Maurya empire the author refers to the large scale land clearance leading to deforestation which meant 'increasing floods damaging the crops, and hence a complete loss of revenue as well as a drain of the state finance for relief measure' (p.110). He is conscious that 'much of all this may sound conjectural', but even then maintains them.

The author resorts to speculation in reconstructing the history of the Āndhras from the middle of the first millennium B.C. (p.118).

Dr. Jha is at pains to disprove 'the much trumpeted notion' of the 'truly democratic' character of the non-monarchical states of the post-Vedic period, applying the strict and absolute definition of democracy of modern times, without considering the historical comparison of other periods and countries (pp.90-91). He refers to 'the strict control which non-monarchical governments exercised over their domains through executive edicts and legislation and to the laws enacted by them 'to control the private and family life of individual members of society'. 'This anticipates the authoritarianism and centralized monarchical governance associated with the Maurya Kings' According to the author, 'they could not do away with the essential organizational and ideological features of the monarchies' and 'possessed all the paraphernalia of a monarchical state apparatus'. He does not refer to the composition of these states, the procedure followed in the deliberations of their assemblies, their judicial system, social and economic life, and to the evidence of the Buddhist and Jain literature, the *Mahābhārata* and the *Arthaśāstra*.

The evaluation of Aśoka's *dhamma* is amusingly novel (pp.105-6) and, without expressly saying so, puts it on the same footing as Akbar's *Din-i-Ilahi*, as criticised by some historians. Its emphasis on toleration of religious eclecticism and Asoka's insistence on suppression of free expression of difference of opinion, it is asserted, were intended to preserve the unity of the vast empire. The author is sceptical and apprehensive, possibly influenced by modern practices, when he says that Aśoka 'banned festive meetings or gathering perhaps due to his fear of conflicts arising out of differences of opinion, only those sponsored by the state seem to have been permissible ... Popular meetings could be utilized to criticize and attack the king's new ideas. Their suppression therefore seems to have been intended to stifle popular opposition' (p.100).

Dr. Jha interprets Aśoka's attack on ritual and sacrifice as intended to undermine the influence of the priest (p.100). This ill suits Aśoka's avowed advocacy of a seemly behaviour and liberality to Brāhmaṇas.

Later the author dismisses Kanishka's patronage of Buddhism also as essentially political, or course without adducing any evidence, but, he asserts that, besides the Buddhist emblems on his coins and the Buddhist legends about him, 'there is very little evidence to suggest that his conversion to Buddhism was a profound experience' (p.116).

The author asserts that 'in the first two centuries of the Christian era, the rulers could not ignore the merchant guilds (*nigama sabhā*) in the towns of the Deccan, though clear proof of their actual participation in administration is lacking' (p.129).

He makes a very definitive statement, again without citing any evidence in his support, that 'most *shudras* seathed in discontent. It is not unlikely that they often turned against brahmanas and other higher castes and caused tension in society' and goes on to add that the law-givers 'provided a number of safeguards against shudra hostility' (p.130).

He explains 'the stringent legal injunctions' of Manu as 'an effort to protect a traditional *varṇa* order now in close contact with alien peoples' (the Yavanas) (p.131). This would involve chronological considerations of the close contact and the date of the text and a reference in it to the objectionable practices of the alien people.

The author evinces admirable ingenuity of speculation when he infers from 'inner compartments without light or ventilation' and outer cells having 'strong wooden doors which could be barred from within and locked from without' that the *Vihāras* at Karle and several other places in the Deccan had precious goods for safe-keeping (p.133).

According to Dr. Jha, the Mahāyanā Buddhism derived its Concept of Maitreya Buddha from the idea of the 'suffering saviour' current in West Asia (p.134). Such cultural borrowings to be accepted as historical facts require certain prerequisite conditions to be fulfilled; mere similarity is not enough.

The remark that 'the science of medicine benefited much from India's contacts with the Western World' (p.146), if intended to imply Western influence on Charaka and Suśruta, is a hangover of 'colonialist imperialist' historians, because historical studies of Indian medicine have demonstrated that the influence was more in the reverse direction.

Dr. Jha is of the view that the Guptas did not possess a large professional army, did not enjoy a monopoly of elephants and horses, and troops supplied by the feudatories constituted the major portion of their army. He refers to the silence on the part of the Allahabad Pillar Inscription and Fa-Hsien. But negative evidence or absence of a reference can be conclusive only when it is demonstrated that the context necessitated its mention.

The author takes a reference in the *Anuśāsanaparva* of the *Mahābhārata*, an unnamed contemporary work, and the legal texts as suggesting a conflict between the Sudras and the ruling classes, but the evidence is not convincing, and he has to admit that 'references to actual revolt by the shudras against the upper classes are not recorded in the sources of the Gupta period' (p.161).

The effects of painstaking arguments are most forcefully applied to the task of demolishing the image of the Gupta period as the golden age (ch.8). The author rightly criticises it for being described as one of 'Hindu renaissance'. The label of 'Indian renaissance' was suggested by early Western scholars, who considered the cultural developments as a rebirth caused by the impetus provided by Greek contact, similar to European renaissance. The controversy about designating it as 'Hindu' is unnecessary and is caused by the ignorant confusion about the history of the use of the term.

Likewise, the discussion about the period being one of 'revival of nationalism' is not to the point, considering the fact that the modern concept of nationalism is a nineteenth century development in European history. It may, however, be noted that the Gupta kings are known to have fought against foreign dynasties. Samudragupta had subdued several foreign rulers mentioned as *Daivaputraṣahaiṣāhānuṣāhi* and *Śakamuruṇḍa*. Chandragupta II destroyed the Saka Kṣatrapa rulers of Gujarat and Kathiawad. In the Meharauli Pillar Inscription king Chandra is said to have defeated the Bāhlikas after crossing the seven rivers, including the Indus. The tradition of Vikramāditya, the vanquisher of the outlandish Śakas is sometimes taken to reflect the achievements of Gupta kings. Skandagupta, in the early years of his reign, rolled back the invasion of the Hūṇas, who carried fire and sword up to Europe, and took steps to strengthen the administrative set-up in the western part of his empire. A later member of the dynasty, Narasiṃhagupta Bālāditya, is said to have defeated the mighty Hūṇa ruler Mihirakula.

The author himself has noticed the remarkable development of architecture, plastic arts, painting, literature of different categories, science and philosophical systems (pp. 162-72). There was an atmosphere of religious harmony and toleration. In many spheres of culture the period witnessed unprecedented efflorescence, carrying forward earlier beginnings and setting classical patterns followed in later ages. All this development requires as a pre-requisite an atmosphere of peace and contentment. The efficient and well-organized administrative system and a long line of very able and active rulers contributed to it. The high metallic value and unmatched artistic excellence of the gold coins of the Guptas symbolise the all round peace and cultural achievements of the period. The unequivocal testimony of Fa-hsien in the fifth century about the general happiness of the people is, the 'upper classes' who were 'happy and prosperous, and lived in comfort and ease' (p.173).

Dr. Jha correctly emphasises the truism that 'the truly golden age of the people does not lie in the past, but in the future'. There has never been a golden age in the past, nor does it occur even in modern times in any of countries with diverse systems of government and policies of public welfare. What to say of the Western countries with various shades of capitalism and socialism, the experiments at materialising the 'much trumpeted' prophecy of golden age of equality and happiness in the Soviet lands has strangely ended in a fiasco and no where else does it promise to be in the process of being realised. Students of history often use the label of 'golden age' in the relative terms with all its limitations. This has been applied, among others, to the periods of Pericles, Augustus, Elizabeth, Victoria and Shahjahan. The golden age is a comparative historical idea considering other periods and countries.

Dr. Jha labours hard to identify dark elements in the social realities of the period. In the process he blows up a few minor points, as interpreted by him, and refers to some evidence pertaining to developments characteristic of later period, which creates chronological confusion and casts false shadow of doubt on the Gupta period. According to him, the land and village grants weakened the royal authority and led to the oppression of peasants and other inhabitants. But, he himself admits that there are very few such grants of the Guptas and that they were made in favour of State officers from the seventh-eighth centuries onwards. He refers to the emergence of feudalism, but clear epigraphic references from Gujarat, Central India, Orissa and Assam to peasants resembling serfs (or villeins) date from the tenth century. His statement that from the Gupta period onwards forced labour was extended to all classes of subjects, and came to include all kinds of work is based on a wrong interpretation of evidence and of the nature of *Viṣṭi* in earlier periods. The evidence for peasant protest against 'feudal agrarian relations and forms of exploitation' is available only from ninth-tenth centuries onwards.

The long distance trade continued to be of interest and concern. In the west Rome was replaced by the Byzantine empire and trade with South-east Asia increased in volume. The connected inland trade was not affected. The excellence of the products of artisans and craftsmen is evidenced. Guilds of artisans and merchants were also active and effective. The view about the paucity of metal money is misconceived; the reference to the use of cowrises, which are known to have been in circulation up to the beginning of the twentieth century, shows low prices of commodities and not paucity of coins.

The theory of 'urban decay' is an oversimplification of the archaeological evidence. At places the decay is noticed from the third-fourth century. In the period archaeologically many towns are evidenced in different parts. This is confirmed by the accounts of the Chinese travellers, epigraphic records and contemporary literature. The *Kāmasūtra* testifies that city culture was a prominent feature of the social life of the period.

The author says that the status of women continued to decline; there was a proliferation of castes including the *Kāyasthas* and the *mahattaras*; there was a pronounced *Varṇa* distinction in various spheres of life; and the ruling class often used religion for maintaining the social order based on *Varṇa*. Evidence associating these developments with the

Gupta period is not so definitive as is suggested.

Within the limited space of review it is not possible to attempt an analysis of the various views expressed in the book. When *Bhakti* (devotion) is described as 'reflecting the complete dependence of the serfs or tenants on the landowners in the context of Indian feudal society' (p.25), it involves a chronological mix-up about the origin and early history of *Bhakti*, the evidence for feudalism and the presence of serfs in the Indian context. Likewise, without noting the chronological hiatus between the archaeological evidence for the regular use of iron for making tools and weapons and the suggested date for large scale clearance of forests by cutting, the author makes a sweeping attack on those who oppose this view by giving them 'a bad name' : 'On this basis the importance of iron technology in facilitating the clearance of land has altogether been denied by some scholars who see no relationship between technological development and social change' (p.53). In p.100 a similar criticism occurs of those who do not subscribe to the view about the various changes attributed to the intensive use of iron: 'who benefit from an advanced technology only to deliberately ignore its significance'.

In a work of this nature the chances of factual mistakes are not expected to occur. For example, *niyoga* is translated as re-marriage of widows, rājasūya as the coronation ceremony (which is only one of the many parts of the sacrifice) (p.56), and *vājapeya* as 'drink of strength' (p.59). Not all the punch-marked coins were issued by merchants as has been stated (p.66). The outstanding contributions of D.D. Kosambi to numismatics include the identification of series of punch-marked coins with particular: kingdoms, dynasties and kings. A *bhogagāma* is explained as a village whose revenues is granted to a *seṭṭhi* for his maintenance (p.68). The author translates *mahājanapada* as a large state and *janapada* as an agricultural settlement (p.78). He does not locate Pāvā of the Mallas in the vicinity of Gorakhpur, but identifies it with Pawapuri in Patna district (p.69). Seniya, another name of Bimbisāra, is translated to mean with an army and is taken to suggest that he was 'perhaps the first king to have a regular standing army' (p.81). But the form of the name is Śeṇiya, Śreṇiya, Srenika and Śreṇya, which has hardly any reference to army.

At places the author makes opposite statements. Though he mentions 'the theory of the base birth of Chandragupta Maurya as no longer acceptable', he says that the prevalent view is that his caste was low (p.93). A similar contradiction appears about the kingdom of Bindusāra extending up to Mysore (pp. 93-95) and Aśoka's missions to Khotan in Central Asia (p.95).

On the authority of Patañjali the author mentions the Maurya practice of establishing cults for the sake of money (p.100). *Arcā* used in the original (p.479; on V.3.99) signifies an idol or image for in the (*pūjārthāḥ*) worship. The passage records a tradition that for the sake of money the Maurya kings made idols (*archāḥ prakalpitāḥ*).

Dr. Jha refers to the threat to the Maurya empire after Aśoka from the south posed by the Āndhras or Sātavāhanas (p.109). But, the rise of the later cannot be pushed back to such an early period.

For the mistakes and wrong interpretations of ancient Indian history the author broadly classifies historians responsible into two groups: colonialist-imperialist and nationalist-revivalist. He is so much obsessed with this idea that at times he imagines their shadowy existence. in the introductory chapter he exposes the defects in the historical writings produced by these two groups. At places he does not notice the growth in historical knowledge with the availability of new material, and sees their hand. The expansion in the geographical horizon of the Harappan culture is marginalised by the remark that 'the Hindu revivalists are busy locating the epicentre of this culture in the elusive Saraswati' (p.30). His remark about a non-academic common man reacting to the historical facts is amusing : 'if a communalist Hindu is told that all his ancestors did not practice cremation (he) may well jump down our throat (p.39). He interprets 'overemphasis on the alleged decentralized nature of the Maurya administration' as 'perhaps rooted in the neocolonialist ideas invading Indian historiography in recent years (p.101).

Dr. Jha rightly feels concerned about the controversy about the final disappearance of the Harappan culture by the Aryan invasion (*c.* 1500 B.C.) being informed by political consideration and its use by social and political activists. His comments mean an unkind reflection on Indian archaeologists, who according to him, did not challenge Sir Mortimar Wheeler's thesis in his lifetime, but, after his death, have criticised it 'with a vengeance as it were' (p.41). Dr. jha himself knows that the Harappan cities seem to have been finally deserted by 1800 B.C. There is enough evidence for the diffusion, expansion and gradual dispersal of the Harappan culture. The evidence pointed out does not show any trace of violent destruction. If, as mentioned by Dr. Jha, the concept of an Aryan race is a myth, then there should be no reliance on a suggested Aryan invasion. Many more cogent causes are considered to have been operative in the case of the Harappan culture. This is the view of many non-Indian scholars also. Advances in our knowledge during several decades have caused this revaluation of the problem, which is not to be connected with the life and death of Sir Wheeler.

History is to be meaningful. This leads to the identification of models. The theoretical formulations often involve ideological commitments. The author is frankly conscious of it when he points out that the account is criticised as being 'too much red' (p.25). Conclusions indicated by research studies are to be welcomed, but, if the researches are done to prove a pre-conceived formulation, then they take away the charm and zest of historical pursuit. A historian is free to pursue his methodology and approach, but he has to grant the same freedom to other co-workers. Condemning others for what he claims to be virtue in his own case would betray: a fascist thinking.

Dr. Jha had done well to present the history by emphasising elements of change and continuity in society and economy, social tensions, mechanisms of exploitation, and the social role of religion and superstition. This draws attention to those aspects of Indian civilization which are often ignored. But, in the process the effort has tended to ignore other aspects. In reaction it ignores aspects which are by no means less important. It creates a wrong impression by sacrificing the whole at the cost of a minor part. The lopsided emphasis is misconceived and gives a distorted picture projected through a jaundiced vision. The beginner and the common man who do not have the occasion to know Indian history in its variety and totality, may not get a chance to view the historical facts in their holistic nature, if they are clouded by a determined effort to fulfill ideological commitments, as contrasted with the loyalty to the discipline of historical science. The academic exercise does not stop with a thesis or an antithesis; it has to proceed forward to its logical and of taking note of the synthesis also. It is not conflict and tension which alone are real; the efforts at harmony and compromise are equally real.

The present monograph is a fine specimen of a systematic presentation of the history of ancient India according to a particular approach. On account of its partial treatment it does not oust and replace many other books with a fuller and more comprehensive coverage. The present work has a limited purpose; it cannot serve as a base book to introduce ancient India in its multi-dimensional personality.

A remarkable development of modern times is the replacement of the puritan academician, engrossed with the technical details of his narrow specialisation be an activitist academician alive to the needs of harnessing the knowledge of his discipline to the problems and realities of his own times. It is, however, another thing if he chooses to drag facts of ancient Indian history to make them relevant to a modern situation not being discussed by him. Thus, in referring to a statement in the Smrti attributed to Manu about the ownership of a piece of unclaimed land, the author points out that Manu's injunctions 'have influenced Indian society for centuries and have created a ferment in our own times' (p.123).

We have already referred to some of the many passages where the author speaks of the social tension between the Śūdras and the first two castes without pointing out any evidence to support his speculation.

The author does not lose any opportunity to refer to events of modern Indian politics, even though the narrative of the ancient period does not require them, especially within the limited scope of a work of the present dimension. He mentions the two events of the assassination of Mahatma Gandhi and the demolition of the Babri Masjid at Ayodhya as unfolding 'the backward-looking Hindu revivalist and fascist politics of contemporary India' (p.23). In referring to the kingdom of Kosala in the later Vedic period, he inserts the remark that 'in our own times his (Rāma's) overzealous devotees have unashamedly politicized him to damage the social fabric of India' (p.57). In the brief reference to the *mahājanapada* of *Kāsī* he mentions that Rāma was not a king of Ayodhyā 'where his modern devotees (*Rāmabhaktas*) demolished a medieval mosque leading to a communal holocaust in the country' (p.78).

According to Dr. Jha, the cow became an object of worship in the post-Maurya period. In his typical style he adds the comment : 'the seeds of communal Indian politics were thus sown' (p.136).

His remarks about the *Gītā* are equally informative. At one place he refers to it as 'the most popular religious text of the upper caste Hindus' (p.17), which, though in Sanskrit, is available in translations in all the regional languages of India. His serious concern for the text is clear in his remark: 'In our own times it is talked about more often than read, its glaring contradictions and poetic excellence being conveniently ignored by those who tirelessly swear by it.' (p.137).

Dr. Jha seems to be motivated by the concern for modern political issues, when, in describing the development of sculpture at Mathurā, he adds the information that it had not yet become 'the home town of the many-faceted Krishna' (p.143). It is interesting to find that Kṛṣṇa had 'deservingly' earned several compliments from the author (p.80 - the numerous layers of contradictory myths that grew around him; p.104 - many-faceted Krishna of later legends; p.135-who is mentioned in the *Rigveda* as a demon and enemy of Indra... pulling strings offstage most of the time in the *Mahabharata*; p.137-his rather questionable personal track record.

9, Gurudham Colony, **Lallanji Gopal**
Varanasi 221010

Rajesh Kochhar, *The Vedic People*, Orient and Longman, 2000, PP.259 Rs. 425.

Dr. Kochhar is a scholar with interest in many areas. He has been a visiting professor at Cambridge and a professor of astrophysics at home. He has been recipient of Nehru Fellowship on a subject not related to science. He has devoted enough time to the study of Purāṇas to write a book on Vedic history.

A man from a different discipline raises our expectations. He has some new and quite different ideas that compel him to intervene into a field which is not his own. Ironically, the central idea in his case is not new but bizarre. He tells us that the Vedic people lived on the banks of a different Sarasvati; they knew a different Gangā and a different Jamunā; a different sea and a different Vindhya; a different Daśarath, a different Sarayū; a different Rāma and a different Ayodhyā. They all are traced in Afghanistan and eastern Iran. Dr Kochhar has definitely written a different history of the Vedic people relying on a non-Vedic source. His merit lies in his determination of time of Vedāṅga Jyotish which may appear fantastic to some and absurd to others. His arguments are mostly ingenuous. "The Arghandab can be equated with Dṛsadvatī and, say, the Tarnak with Apaya. There have already been suggestions that Ārjikīyā be identified with the Arghastan. Lakes like Śaryaṇavant and Anyatahplakṣa can easily be placed in the hilly area of Koh-i-Baba from where the Hilmand starts."

The possibility of Afghanistan as the locale of VI *maṇḍala* of Ṛgveda was discussed more persuasively and far less inconsistently in the nineteenth and early twentieth centuries and rejected even by other protagonists of the Aryan invasion hypothesis. The chorus, that part of Ṛgveda is not Indo-Aryan but Indo-European document cheered many but died silently. Its echoes remained in outdated books to entertain the credulous ones. Kosambi thought some of the verses, even of the X *maṇḍala,* were written in Mesopotamia; Kochhar revives Hillebrandt with a new abracadabra.

Dr. Kochhar starts his book in a philosophical muse, "There are, however, certain intrinsic difficulties associated with examining the past. First, the past does not have an independent existence. Even though the past precedes the present, it can exist only in the context of the present. The only look permitted at the past is a flashback."

As we know, no period of time has an 'independent' existence. In circular logic, one may as well say that the present can exist only in the context of the past. We know the present when it has become the real past, which we call the *present perfect.* It is only past which has a veritable presence. The present in its absolute present-ness has a notional existence. We face the present with the past beside and inside us - in our accumulated knowledge and experience, our long cherished dreams, and the infra-structure and super-structure that has been handed down to us.

He laments, "There are, however, no objective criterion to define historical grain vis-a-vis historical chaff and separate the two." Separation of the truth from half-truths is no less difficult in case of the present. Even in the case of present, we are right or wrong within the scope of information available to us.

Dr. Kochhar makes some observations on the nature of Time as well. "Time is one way street. We are permitted to turn our neck and look back, but we are not permitted a U-turn." His spatial vision does not allow him to see the present-ness of the past and past-ness of the present. Whatever we have from the past - object, artifact, text, lore, fossil, ash, charcoal, geological signatures - exists here and now. We study the present with better understanding and more sophisticated tools to know the past. There is no point in looking back, no one can do that, except in space where one may expect to see the past in future. Spatial description of time is misplaced poetry. It is not an arrow, not a wheel, not a street, not a stream, not a sea and yet it is all and inconceivably much more to defy spatial categories. Time must be understood as time alone - without simile and epithet. What is enigmatic with Dr. Kochhar is that he takes his poetry too seriously.

A scholar of natural sciences, Dr. Kochhar is slightly less equipped to do justice to history. He does not understand its nature. He feels uncomfortable because of the lack of laboratory facilities or a modern observatory for the study of history to catch *the original signals* from Puranic hodge-podge.

In his opinion, "Purāṇas are like an audio cassette, which has been dubbed and re-dubbed so many times that it is not an easy task to separate the original 'signal' from the accumulated noise." But it is the re-dubbed audiocassette, which helps him fix the date of Ṛksamhitā at c. 900 BC. He himself explains:

"Content of the Purāṇas was twisted out of shape. Kings and their dynasties were intermixed; *ṛṣis* and gods freely interacted with the kings...Confusion has also been caused by similarity of names which belonged to different dynasties or which were far removed from each other in time." (p.29) Nevertheless, he constantly refers to the Purāṇas and epics and, to describe the Vedic people.

We are of the view that no source is forbidden for detection of truth. Even gossips and rumours can be sources of history and criminal investigation. But one must have the necessary acumen. Dr. Kochhar lacks it.

A common culture prevailed from India to Europe and one language spread across this vast space. The central issue is that of direction of the flow. Dr Kochhar supports the northwest to southeast hypothesis and so Afghanistan first, India next.

His book is laced with intermittent hints and suggestions on methodology. So, a brief on the art of separating the grain from the chaff, or, as Dr. Kochhar alternately says, the art of picking the right signal from the noise, may not be out of place.

The first task in such cases is to isolate one signal from the other, the recurring one from the casual, the neutral one from the tainted, and then, in the last case, to read the motive behind the taint and remove the taint to render it plain. The next task is that of decoding the signals, i.e., to understand the implication behind the allegories and statements. The third stage is that of comparison and cross-examination. This exercise must precede the ensuing conclusions.

Coming to Purāṇas and Epics we have two types of noises. One is accordant, the other discordant. The first is general, much like a running theme, the second a freak. The latter should be checked to see if it fits well within the general scheme or not. If not, it may be cosmetic interpolation.

As far Afghanistan and BMRC (Bactria-Margiana-Complex) are concerned, the theme song of the Epics and Purāṇas is that the condemned and befallen progeny of Viśvāmitra peoples them. They are all Kṣhatriyas, who have lost their caste status.

On decoding this allusion we read: there is an Indian component among the Afghans (Darda), Bactrians (Vahikas/ Vahlikas), Iranians (Parshava, Pahlavas, Pardas), and Central Asians and western Chinese (Shakas, Magas, Mandagas, Hūṇas, Chīnās).

We, thus find the strongest Purāṇic signal vindicated by history, archaeology and linguistics. It is a good case to be examined in detail.

Secondly, Purāṇas and Epics knew Central Asia as Uttara Kuru and Śakadvīpa. Kuru without qualifier was in Haryana and Kuru with a qualifier covered Central Asia. This, in Purāṇic sources, is a clinching evidence to show that the flow was in the opposite direction. Look at the analogies: England - New England, York - New York, Jersey- New Jersey, Wales -South Wales - New South Wales, Mexico - New Mexico, Ireland - New Ireland (in Pacific), Indies - West Indies, Bengal - West Bengal. Bombay - New Bombay. The old and the original one needs no qualifier. The same name with qualifier suggests that it was created later or the people there had come from the one without qualifier. Geographical names never betray us. There is no exception.

So their first assertion that the tribes outside are the condemned children of Viśvāmitra, or a strain originating from India settled and merged in the local population there, stands vindicated by the geographical name. This may be a good indicator as to which Sarasvatī could have been the original and which one later.

Thirdly, the countries beyond the Himalayas are viewed as paradise. No country dubbed its own home as paradise. It is the other one. It can not be even the old home. Old home is holy, but not paradise. This paradise is unholy. People who visited it compromised their caste status, as they came in contact with the defiled ones living in those lands. In this paradise those who had been charitable enjoyed a life of license and plenty and lived in adequately guarded and fortified areas, which did not permit easy entry to the outsiders. Allusions are unmistakable as they say that the *devas* lived here on this very soil and from here they went to the paradise and enroute they felt threatened that the *asuras* might harm them. Even their fortified paradise was seized and threatened. SOS messages were sent and immediate enforcement dispatched from the mainland. It was the movement to and from these centers that prompted the poets to create a world of mutual dependence and easy communion between the mortals and the immortals. Even the contradictions within this belief are indicative of a thin but incessant migration of affluent ones from the mainland to the other one. Fortified Aryan habitations have been identified by scholars throughout this cultural complex.

Now we may check whether apparently discordant notes fit into this scheme or not. Dr. Kochhar informs us:

(1) "*Zoroastrian literature clearly points towards Central Asia being the original home of Iranians.* In view of the extremely close relationship between the Rgveda and the Avesta, Central Asia must be accepted as the habitat of the Indo-Aryans also." (p.95)

(2) "*Yasna 10.10. Haraiti Bareza (also called Har Baraziti as Soma habitat. Haraiti is identified with Mount Elburz.* But it must be borne in mind that the name Elburz not only denoted the present Mount Elburz, a peak in Caucasus, but was also applied to the whole range of mountains extending from the Hindu Kush in the East to the Caucasus in the west." (p.100)

(3) "*The Rgveda does not contain any hymns that refer to the Aryan homeland and the migration from it...* The absence of evidence does not constitute evidence of absence." (p.93)

(4) "*One may add that a reader depending entirely on internal evidence in the Rgveda would not learn about the existence of the related text of the Avesta.* It would thus seem that it was not the intention of the Rgvedic authors to prepare a gazetteer of their life and times." (p.11)

(5) "*The weight of evidence now available goes against the invasion hypothesis. The idea has however persisted and has been met with the counter idea that the Aryans themselves have been Harappans.* The counter-idea can be sustained only by a wholesale rejection of evidence to the contrary." (p.14)

(6) "*...many Rgvedic clan names are phonetically similar to the old Iranian names preserved by Greek historians: Pārāvata, Kāmboja, Parśu, Pārthava, Sṛjaya, and others.*"

We have emphasized the factual statement. They mutually vindicate each other and collectively vindicate the conclusion arrived at by us.

The non-emphasized part consists of persuasive pleas by Dr. Kochhar to divert the attention from the direct import of the facts. They all militate against invasion/ migration thesis.

Now we take the seemingly freak notes, which show presence of some Vedic or Purāṇic luminaries in Afghanistan. Should they not be there when they are very much there? In Vedic accounts Viśvāmitra is the priest of Bharatas, and is perhaps replaced by Vaśiṣṭha. In one verse he is shown on the confluence of Vyāsa and Satluj. Dr. Kochhar notes:

"If Viśvāmitra arrived there with car and wagon, it must be entourage's first crossing of the rivers. Significantly, Viśvāmitra addresses Vipās first, implying that he was parked to its west. There is however a curious element. If Viśvāmitra was crossing the rivers for the first time, how did he know that the two rivers reach the ocean?" (p.126)

Naturally, Visvamitra is neither an intruder nor an Arayan invader. He not only knew that the two rivers met the sea, he also knows they rise from the same mountain. He is engaged in some business in which one has often to cross the rivers, which fall on his route. In passing it may be pointed out that too much is read in simple statements to create evidence. The poet does not address Vipās first and Śutudri later. He addresses both at the same time - as Vipāp-Śutudri. It is simply metric compulsion that Vipās comes first. There is nothing to suggest that he is coming from west to east.

In Purāṇic and Epic accounts there is a deliberate attempt to berate Viśvāmitra in many ways. He is a tantric who creates a parallel creation; a king *ṛṣi*, *rājarṣi*, who aspires to become *brahmarṣi* ; a *ṛṣi* who had his *āśrama* at the bank of Kosi in Bihar and a *ṛṣi* who achieves his Brāhmaṇhood in a scenario which reminds Dr. Kochhar of Seistan.

"...a couple of Puranic accounts that match the Seistan locale... an early Ikṣvāku king, Kuvalāśva, killed a rākṣasa named Dhundhu near a sand-filled sea called Ujjalaka. Viśvāmitra is said to have attained brahmanhood at Ruṣangu tīrtha that is described as being on the bank of river Sarasvatī and in the lowlands near the sea (sāgarnūpe). (p.131)

Firstly, there is nothing to preclude Rann from the Ujjalaka Sea on the mouth of Sarasvatī. But suppose we accept the suggestion thrown by Dr. Kochhar, we may ask, 'what is wrong if an Indian luminary known for his movement to and fro, is found anywhere within the Harappan contact area or the area covered by the Purāṇic accounts.

II

The book is full of inconsistencies. The first inconsistency starts with the title itself. The book entitled *The Vedic People*, does not tell anything about the Vedic people, nor does it use the Vedic sources. It should have been titled *The Puranic People*. But there again is a flaw. It does not discuss anything about the society, i.e., the people - their economy, their industry, their culture, their language (which should have been closer to Vālmīkīya Sanskrit), or their avocations - except their lineage and abode. Its sole purpose lies in proving that the Vedic people came to India from outside. So *Early Abode of the Aryans as seen from Puranic Accounts by an Astrophysicist* could be more appropriate. But it was far too long for the title. So a shorter title *Encounter of Dr. Kochhar with Vedic Afghans* is recommended as a middle course.

Dr. Kochhar succumbs in his introductory pages (p.10) itself, when he states "This joint Indo-European homeland was correctly placed after a number of false starts in the Eurasian steppes." The basic task of the author is complete before the inquiry starts. What remains is the small task of forging a well- trimmed packing case that consumes twenty five times of additional written space.

Dr. Kochhar is capable of creating chaos out of an order. As we have noted he is of the opinion that 'Rgveda was compiled in 900 BC.'

"...that the battle (Mahabharata) took place in about 900 BC. This would also be the Puranic date for final compilation of the Ṛgveda.... this date is quite close to the date of 1000 BC that has been arrived at for the Ṛgveda from entirely different route, that is a comparison of the structure of the Ṛgvedic language with that of the later texts" (p.53).

Vedāṅga Jyotiṣa, according to him deserves to be placed at 1400 BC. His argument is notable:

"Vedanga ... comes in two recensions: Ṛgvedic and Yajurvedic. The Rgvedic recension consists of 36 verses. Thirty of these are repeated in Yajurvedic. recension which in turn contains additional 13 verses. There are thus in all 46 astronomical verses, some of which have not yet been interpreted. The Ṛgvedic recension is attributed to Lagadh. *Vedāṅga Jyotiṣa* has been placed at about 1400 BC."

"Verses 7 and 22 of the Rv. version say that the duration of the longest day, that is summer solstice, is 18 muhurtas (1 day = 30 m.). Thus the ratio of the longest day to the shortest night is 3:2. This statement is repeated in other texts also, for example in Kautilyas Arthśāstra and Pātanjali's Mahābhāṣya. Later the ratio was spotted by Babylonians about 700 BC."

"A simple mathematical calculation shows that the Vedāṇga Jyotiṣa statement correspondes to a rather northerly latitude of 35ĽN. To get an idea of this location, note that Shrinagar, Herat and Kabul all are at about 34ĻN." (p.112-113).

What makes it self-defeating is his dating of the Ṛksamhitā. How could Vedāṅgas (explanatory exercises) have developed in the absence of the Saṁhitā? Inspired by which *ṛṣi's* hymns? He knows that the Veda comes into existence as and when it was compiled as a Saṁhitā. Prior to that, there were only the hymns and *ṛks,* scattered in priestly families. So he admits by default that the compilation of all the Vedas had taken place much earlier than 1400 BC.

By 1400 BC Afghanistan had been so deeply Aryanised that there were centres of learning in Afghanistan and original works in Sanskrit were being written in Afghanistan. According to Bhaviṣya Purāṇa all the four Vedas were available in Central Asia (among the Magas) as well, but in somewhat corrupt form. They emulated the *varṇa vibhāga,* social division among them - Brahmins were Magas, Ksatriyas : Magadha, Vaiśyas : Manasas, and Shūdras : Mandaga - but in the eyes of Indians they all were deemed to have lost their social status and acquired, *vṛiṣalatva,* hybridization. This social division was emulated among some European IE speakers as well. So we have a perfect corroboration from many angles.

Dr. Kochhar knows and admits that the Veda is like a wax record, true to the original. We have nothing to complain why he does not make sensible use of this authentic source; but the odd thing with him is that he lifts the Purāṇa out of the Vedas. "There must therefore have been an independent databank for the Vedic authors to draw from" (p.30). This observation is correct and so is his inference, "While the Puranic databank fed information to the Vedic texts, there was also a reverse process in action" (p.30). But the question is what device has the author evolved to reach that independent databank? None. On the contrary, by his mix up he creates space for pick and choose and free play of imagination.

An author who claims any area to be the habitat of a people must pin point the area and archaeological assemblage with which he associates them. Dr. Kochhar solves the problem in a ridiculous way:

"The problem is made worse by the fact that in the era of Vedic studies no archaeological data are available". (p.12).

One may ask, why? Why the archaeology of a people, who used more than 37 types of utensils, a wide range of implements, weaponry and ornaments, identical to the ones used by Harappans, should disappear from all the regions, identified by scholars either as original habitat or secondary homes? Denial of their archaeology can have no other justification except perpetration of a lie for something sinister. Had he not been mesmerized by the *akhaṇḍa pāṭha* of Aryan invasion, Kochhar, with his scientific temper, could have easily detected the ploy. He failed by choice.

Dr. Kochhar makes innovative remarks in semantics as well, "Samskrita literally meaning 'put together'..." (21). Now the next threatened field appears to be linguistics.

It appears incongruous to Dr. Kocchar "when one searches for (and finds!) details of artisanal activities like metallurgy in the priestly literature." and he offers his brief, "Such 'experts' do well to take note of what Sāyaṇa and others had to say of their pre-science age interpretation of the so called 'scientific' passages of the Vedas" (p. 22). It appears, science was born the day Dr. Kochhar was born. It has neither history nor pre-history. We thought science was born the day man started using his hand and mind, and progressed with discernment and discrimination. It has advanced from one revolution to the other. Till the Vedic age scores of revolutions had taken place. To name a few, those of control, preservation and use of fire (physics); cooking and use of recipes (chemistry), use of fertilizer (geology), invention of raft and float (hydrology); firing of ceramic objects, pottery and brick, (chemical engineering) discreet understanding of the components of speech, which was far advanced by the Vedic times (linguistics); observation of the nature of motion and invention of wheels (dynamics), diagnosis of diseases and identifications of medicinal plants and remedies (medical science), observation of stars and heavenly bodies and determination of cycles of time - day, night, fortnight, month, solar cycle, intercalary years (astronomy); meditation on the mode of existence, evolution and ultimate fate of the cosmos (cosmology and astrophysics), understanding the working of mind (psychology), yoga and prāṇāyāma (transcendental psychology), planning of cities, habitations, roads and lanes and drains within habitations and individual structures (geomentry), counting and comprehending the highest denominations (arithmatics) and many more. We only ask, does the professor understand what science is?

Dr. Kochhar is not a Vedic scholar and he definitely does not know what Sāyaṇa has said, and how Sāyaṇa has been interpreted by modern scholars. Being a scientist he should know better that the metal objects could not be produced without some advancement in metallurgy.

The real beauty of Dr. Kochhar is his incoherence. He is seldom conscious of the import of what he writes, 'It appears that copper metallurgy reached (Afghanistan and) Baluchistan in a fully developed form from Iran. Tel-e-Iblis, in the copper-rich Kuhrud Mountain, provides evidence for the sequence of developmental stages in copper technology as early as fifth millennium BC. (Unlike copper, iron technology was indigenously developed in India in about 1000 BC.)' (p. 63-64).

The Dr. is too willing to concede the science of metallurgy in the same Pre-science Age two millennia earlier when it comes to Afghanistan.

How could the Aryans of Dr. Kochhar who lived and composed in Iran and Afghanistan remain ignorant of copper-bronze technology? As far as Indian subcontinent is concerned copper beads appear at Mehragarh A-I, in the seventh millennium BC, almost two millennia earlier than Tel-e-Iblis. We know enough, but not good enough to make definite claims as to who was the leader in metallurgy. The exact mechanism has yet to be known. Kochhar himself forgets his own remarks, "It does not seem to be widely known that Tosham area in Bhiwani district, Haryana, 160 km north northwest of Delhi, contains abundant and easily accessible deposits of primary tin (as cassiterite) as well as copper" (p.70-71). There are other sources in India close by which were exploited in antiquity.

He says, "The strength of the Aryans came from their use of the horse and chariots. The Dāsas and Paṇis must have also been similarly equipped." (p.78)

When both are similarly equipped, where in lies the strength of the Aryans? Dr. Kochhar should find a more plausible answer. His plight lies in his thoughtless repetition of the old song, i.e., superiority of Aryans over Harappans because of their horse and chariot, and sudden realisation that he is talking of Afghanistan, not Indus Valley. We fail to understand, what was the hurry that prompted him to write a book before his ideas got crystallized?

He repeats the opinion popular among a section of European scholars that the old portions, at least the sixth Maṇḍala was written when Indo-Aryans were in northern Afghanistan or its vicinity. Only other Maṇḍalas which include 7th and 4th as well were written in 'India'. Talageri in his book, *The Rigveda - a Historical Analysis* has done a commendable work separating the grain from the chaff, so far as periodisation is concerned. Kochhar could not have any idea of the work as it has been published in 2000 itself.

Kochhar holds Avesta and Ṛgveda to be texts of the same time depth. He needs to be reminded that late portions of Avesta are as late as the 4th century AD.

The difference between Vedic and Zend is that Vedic is spoken language and keeps on changing till Paṇini exercises his authority to make it accessible only to the formally educated. Zend is priestly language, which like exiled Hebrew remained unchanged during its entire history.

Writes James Darmesteter in his introduction to the translation of *Vendidad:*

"Yet great is the value which that small book, the Avesta, and the belief of that scanty people, the Pārsis, have in the eyes of the historian and theologist, as they present to us the last reflex of the ideas which prevailed in Iran during the five centuries which preceded and the seven which followed the birth of Christ" (SBES, Vol. IV, xii).

He makes a more precise remark about the text, "Zend texts may have been composed even as late as the fourth century" (*ibid,* xxxviii).

He is clear that "Zend was not the language of Persia." He further elaborates, 'That language not only was not, but had never been the national language of Persia... the relation between ancient Persian and Zend are of such a kind that neither language can be conceived as derived from the other; they are not as one and the same language at two different stages of development, but two independent dialects in nearly the same stage, which is a proof that they did not belong to the same country, and, therefore, that Zend was not the language of Persia" (*ibid.*xxxvi).

Now, what is the state of the Vedic?

(i) It was spoken in a vast area. Paṇini admits of the existence of dialects (vibhāṣās) in Vedic, which is possible only in one case, i.e., the language was spoken over a vast area.

(ii) Sanskrit, MIA and NIA are all Vedic at different stages of development or degeneration, whatever one chooses to call it. In short, Vedic is the language with strong roots in India, while Zend and its other versions in the adjacent countries are dialects having no local roots; they are colonial languages, spoken by the elite, and through them, exercising an abiding impact on the local languages.

In order to elucidate our point we would like to point out what a real linguistic studies undertaken by Emeneau and others have to say on the problem under their cherished notion that IA is an immigrant language in India. Kuiper 'The genesis of a linguistic area, *Indo-Iranian Journal,* 10, 1967:90-91), is cited by Emeneau, thus:

"...The interpretation of these traits in terms of bilingualism prevailing at a period antedating the earliest textual evidence remains problematical (allowing a different solution in terms of pre-Indo-Aryan development without outside influence), unless correlation is possible with 'similar interpretations of other, apparently contemporary, phenomena."

So, long before the composition of the oldest hymn, even before the emergence of the Vedic in its recorded form, an interaction with the non-Aryan dialects was taking place and thus was shaped the OIA, the Vedic, as we find it recorded in the texts. It was not an intrusive language even though the scholars are baffled by this piquant situation. It must not have been the spoken language in its literary form. Itwas, we guess, the colloquial Vedic of respective areas that migrated from more than one centre, and that is why literary OIA, Vedic, falls slightly short of the expectations of PIE.

Now, we are faced with some interesting points. If Zend is literally the Persian version of Vedic Sanskrit, from which country and at what stage the language migrated to Iran? Definitely, at some stage after the language came to its literary maturity, and definitely at a stage when the Vedic texts had been written/ composed.

Kochhar counsels, "any statement that is made about the history of the Vedic people should not only be consistent with the Vedic texts but also with the Avesta'(p.35). He offers ceremonials and does it with fondness, 'Since all our information comes from linguistic sources, our terminology should also be linguistic. In particular, no racial conclusions should be drawn" (p.37).

He associates the Aryans with PGW people, "Thermoluminence dates from Bhagwanpura suggest that the late Harappan phase (sub-period 1A) lasted from 1700 BC to c. 1300 BC. In about 1400 BC. the plain Grey Ware-using people arrived, who later introduced the Painted Grey Ware." (p.87) But in 1400 BC his Aryans were in Afghanistan writing Vedāṅg Jyotiṣa. They must have completed the book, decided the auspicious muhūrta for entering India and started log stock and barrel.

He is also aware that "There is no material culture that can be explicitly associated with the Ṛgvedic people." So much for their association with PGW.

He retracts time and again, "Some artefacts at the PGW sites are suggestive of rituals described in the *Srautsūtras*." (p.89) What does it signify in terms of the Vedic chronology?

He reiterates much of what has been earlier said on Soma to fortify an Afghanistani abode. Such diversions and dilations in the book are intended to increase the number of pages as he has little to say of his own. He stuffs much rudimentary information culled from other books on Vedic texts but does not mention their relative chronology in order to conceal the fact that the Vedāṅga Jyotiṣ of *Yajurveda* in 1400 BC may place *Yajurveda* much behind that time and Ṛgveda further back, in third millennium.

We agree with Dr. Kochhar that, "The Puranas as we have seen are a curious mix of history, mythology and nonsense. (p.30)" But we must add that so is his book which draws freely from the Purāṇas without knowing how to handle the text. Only scientists with journalistic temptations can write the modern Purāṇas, and that he has done without demur. The most interesting thing about him is that he is not wrong; he is simply incredible.

Bhagwan Singh

S. Manik and S.A. Chanchal, *Vedic History with a Difference,* Dinratri Prakashan, 38/2 Ka Banglabazar, Dhaka 1100, Bangladesh, 1995, pp.167, priced Tk.250, US$15.

Two scholars of Bangladesh Shamsuzzoha Manik and Shamsul Alam Chanchal, published a book *The Aryans and the Indus Civilization,* some five years back, in 1995. They argue that the Harappans were none other than the Ṛigvedic Aryans, who fought amongst themselves on religious differences and that with some other ancillary factors it resulted into decay of the Civilization and dispersal of the people. It is a new thesis indeed. The book is divided in 4 chapters. The first one is a resumé of Harappan civilization, from its inception to finale, the PGW, based on writings of other scholars. It is interspersed with some highlights, "The similarities spread over a vast area. Not only the cities and towns, but the villages also maintained a continuous similarity and common standard and pattern. But archaeological information shows some regional differences in the Early Harappan settlements. These can be seen in the Mature Harappan settlements as well. This regional diversity is visible in ritual objects, deities, fire-altars" (11). "After the decline of the Harappan Civilization the cities and the towns were depopulated and the people dispersed over a large area. The number of small towns and villages increased" (12). "The urban character of the Harappan Civilization disappeared during the Late Harappan period, but some architectural features like building, drains and the platforms continued. The quality of metal objects was maintained the same, but the quantity decreased" (p.13). One may note that they have their angle maintained in presentation of the general features as well.

On the literary side, which is dealt in the second chapter, 'The Ṛgveda and the Indus Society', they note that "The formation of a mature civilization and the composition of a rich religious literature like the Ṛgveda can not be made by a nomadic and warring tribe... A stable life is the first condition for the birth of civilization where different classes in the society like priests, craftsmen, traders, farmers function by maintaining relationship with each other." (p.15-16). They cite relevant verses from the Ṛgveda relating various agricultural activities, and those indicative of craft specialization and production such as weaving, gold-smithy, etc.', and mention the tools and implements, to substantiate that there is nothing discordant which precludes identity of Aryans as Harappans. There is nothing to deny their observation.

The point, which makes this work, a different reading of the Ṛgveda relates to the decay and disintegration of the Harappan civilization, which they perceive in their own way. Here it must be pointed out that this is a pioneer work in its own right. No other scholar had identified Harappan civilization as Ṛigvedic, before the publication of my own work in Hindi (1987) which they could not read and in English (1995) which is the year of publication of this work. Others who rejected the invasion/ migration hypothesis placed Ṛgveda much before the Harappans, who in their reckoning reflected either Yajurvedic society or the one found in Sūtra literature. Those who upheld invasion/migration hypothesis could naturally see nothing in common. They both talked in an archaeological void. The former did not mention it and they do the same ~~even~~ today, the latter declared that the Aryans had everything except archaeology. Another matching point of this book with the Vedic Harappans is that it deals to a reasonable extent with the material aspect of the society which the former found too gross to discuss and the latter dealt primitively. We, therefore, deem it a pioneer attempt to look at the issue from a new angle even though it has some serious limitations.

However, coming to the text and treatment, there is nothing to deny that the Ṛgveda reverberates with encounters with enemies and concern for safety. Religious or ritualistic difference is one of the causes of their social tension. The authors suggest that the enemies are generally abusively called "Dāsa or Dasyu" which they could or could not be. This observation has also its merit as many a tribe were censured for their non-observance of sacrifice and charity to Brahmins alone; "It can be assumed that both the Vedic Aryans and their enemies comprised of many tribes, or nations of different complexions. But there are numerous instances indicating confrontation of Aryans with Aryans, or the situations in which both the sides in their war cry invoke Indra. They produce a list of esteemed Vedic personalities whose kin or namesake are shown as killed by the Aryans. They cite verses in which Aryans fight Aryans.

They adduce their reason to show that both god Indra and Agni are minor gods, "god Indra was not so important before the Vedic war" and "Agni was the first Angiras Rishi". The priests are out to make them important. Here in lies the seed of a reform movement, culminating into a civil war, "the Vedic civil war was a religious war. In this war the Vedic poets, who were the leaders on the Vedic side, carried the religious traditions which were already in fashion in the Greater Indus Valley... if it had not been a religious war, the priests would have no role" (p.37).

Now they introduce the parallels in history, the exodus of the followers of Moses from Egypt and all that is necessary to uphold this proposition. Now come the monotheistic thought of the Vedic poets. Establishing parallel gods was undermining the supremacy of Varuṇa. The allusion that says, Indra killed his father and rendered his mother a widow.

All that can be said of this lengthy discussion is that it is a sincere attempt to understand the degeneration of the Harappan civilization. Their access to the text through translations, recent past experiences of the subcontinent and their upbringing in a theocratic society in which religion and belief are seen in action, combined to drive them to find an answer in civil strife caused by religious differences. There is no disregard or disrespect shown to any religion or sect. On the contrary, they are quite alert not to hurt anyone's sentiments. Monotheism of Indus was not monotheism like Islam, which is violently intolerant and absolutist in nature. An intolerant monotheism must be over centralized, must make the ruler all powerful, must be reflected in centralized capital and large army" (p.54). Scholars have been looking for raid and booty in case of every clash with contending forces. There is therefore no harm if two scholars in their analysis see religious strife and attendant social upheaval behind those allusions especially as strong worded religious censures are found in Ṛgveda aplenty.

As noted by the authors archaeologically there are regional cultures which are precursors to the emerging great culture which spreads and assimilates the regional ones to make them its own sub-cultures. It enriches them and enriches itself. The changes come not because of any aggressive overture to conquer and subjugate the minor cultures and people but progressive acceptance of the dominant culture by the minor cultures, which take pride in having acquired some traits of the higher culture. This process of convergence rather than conversion, is the characteristic feature of Indian civilization. It accommodates rather than eliminates. Now with all the diverse deities finding their place in the pantheon, the deities of the culturally advanced or numerically impressive find greater acceptance while their counterpart enjoys the same supremacy among its adherents. It does not create any problem even though their relative importance is governed by this invisible rivalry of gods, reflective of devotional trends in society. Even today, there may be families in which one member is a Śākta, holding mother goddess to be supreme and the other may be *vaishṇavite* or a Śaiva worshipping any of the many incarnations of the Supreme Being. Ṛgveda acknowledges all the gods the way they are and at the same time says that they are manifestations of the one and the same Supreme Being. This is a concept totally different from monotheism. This is *advaita*, acceptance of everyone at par, existence of the Supreme not yonder and beyond, but everywhere, in everything. Monotheism is negative, exterminating; *advaita* is positive, accommodative and assimilative. This is why scholars coming from monotheistic cultures feel confused why most of the deities share common characteristics. They again get confused why and how position of some gods gets gradually undermined and ultimately they are replaced by new deities. How a god, who was subordinate to Mahā-deva or Mahā-Indra gets promoted over him although in name he is yet only Indra. In fact the old one was himself the Indra, and after the new deity replaced him as Indra, he was promoted to a status which is nominally superior even today, but is undermined status-wise. And then a deity, subordinate to Indra, *upendra*, becomes Visṇu, and Indra is relegated to a minor position. So the competition between Indra and Varuṇa is not eliminative, it is accommodative. It is generally overlooked that not only Varuṇa but Indra as well looses his central authority after the Vedic period. It is not only the Varuṇa devotees who go out to Iran, but also Indra devotees whom we witness in Turkey. And it is also generally forgotten that the same poets sing and praise the two, at times invoking the two in unison.

There are cases of assertion of one deity *vis-a-vis* the other, Maruts *versus* Indra, Vṛṣākapi versus Indra and Aṅgiras versus Indra, Bhārgavas *versus* Viṣṇu. But throughout Indian tradition the two sides command equal respect for the other. Even in the Ṛgveda Indra is conciliatory in all the cases. In practice he gains superiority - Maruts are his allies and Indra their leader; Vṛṣakapi is his son; Aṅgirasas are his allies like the Maruts in Vala episode. How many rain-cum-storm gods have we? The ancient Fire God, Mahesh, replaced by his sons, Rudriyas, who conjointly are the storm-gods of the same numerically dominant, but culturally subservient component. He is not replaced by the god or gods of another culture, but of his own, at a different developmental stage. Only after his progeny are in power, as storm gods, there comes in another sky-god, not exactly the Dyaus-Pitar, but the sub-Dyaus-Pitar, the Varuṇa, who ruled as nocturnal god enjoying equal status with the diurnal god, Mitra. He has his māyā or charm. Mitra is the god of righteousness, the day god, replaced silently by Aryamā. In fact the phenomena is so complex that we feel, we might have done damage to the proper understanding of this intricate issue by our simplistic explanation. Let us therefore submit that whatever I have said above is all only tentative. It can be rejected with scorn by a scholar who attempts an in-depth study and comes to a different conclusion. There was no other way left to us to convince the readers inciuding the authors that a fine thesis has lost much of its charm because of wrong perceptions.

But, at the same time, this is a remarkable book in so far as it breaks free from acquired shackles and investigates with an open mind. Many more such studies are needed before we make definite statements. Meantime we may have some archeological secrets, like Kunal which may demand a revision of our thesis here. It is based on hasty reading of the text, ignorance of other Vedic texts and tentative inferences from archaeological records.

Decay in the Indo-Sarasvati was caused because of many factors of which they are also conscious. One of them may be corresponding decay or disturbance in the countries falling mainly on the land route with which Harappans dealt. This might have been initially slow but gradually aggravated to build into a major crisis. The Kutch and Gujarat Harappans had already appropriated trade with gulf countries.

But the major crisis ensued from meteorological imbalance resulting into uncertain weather with prolonged famine with occasional inundation and a protracted dry spell for centuries. This has been recorded both in *Mahābhārat* and in the Vedic context with all its horrors and *Śatapatha Brāhmaṇ* (I.4.1)Videgha Madhava episode. *Mahābhārat* (*Śantiparva*.141-43) gives a complete account of the decay and desertion of urban civilization.

During this period survival became the foremost challenge. Pressure increased on agriculture and settlements were brought precariously close to water sources. Clashes for land gathered alarming proportion. Social status of traders was seriously undermined. Even the Brahmins lost some of their charm as they had no explanation for the failure of their *yajña* in causing rain. Khatriyas, the arm-wielding class ,became most powerful. Even some of the Brahmins took to arm as we find in Mahābhārat. *Aśvamedha* and *rājasūya* were performed to annex land from neighbours. This is the period immediately preceding PGW and initial stage of Grey Ware when a large amount of rough hand made pottery replaces the Harappan ware. This is reflective of the tragedy that even skilled workers had to ignore their family trade. Weapons were more in demand so copper-smithy had not to suffer as much but ore-extraction or say, mining suffered. The *Mahābhārat* is the lone faithful record of this crisis in which all bonds and values suffer in a cry for maintaining them at some cost. In fact mature PGW with its deluxe pottery may be seen as a relief and recovery. This is a scene I can build on the basis of literature. How much do geological studies and archaeological records support it, it is up to them experts. At least there was no movement in late Harappan period towards the west. It was towards east, north and south.

Bhagwan Singh, *The Vedic Harappans* Delhi: Aditya Prakashan, 1995, pp. 493. Price Rs. 850/-

For some champions of Hinduism, India is a Hindu nation and therefore it's greatness has to derive from the Aryans. This naturally requires that the Aryans be at least local residents and not intruders from outside. These individuals are not bothered by the fact that India is itself a constantly changing geographical entity, and going further into the geological past, even the Indian plate has been shifting its loyalty. Although to an archaeologist, it is more important to know the material culture and its superstructure, the identification of the Aryans with a known archaeological assemblage has been an outstanding problem. This issue has recently acquired some political overtones because of the Sangh Parivar's avowed aim of finding an Indian home for the Aryans. If B. Singh were a hard-core member of the Parivar, one would not have spent time reading this book. I was however informed that he has been a Leftist, (who are at least good at arguing their case logically), and this tempted me to read it. For Singh who is only a Hindi fiction writer, this book appears to be a brave excursion into the technical domains of archaeology and philology.

I thought it will be a worthwhile effort to go through this massive book as very often, a scholar from outside the discipline, unconditioned as he is by the axioms of the speciality, is able to provide a new angle, a new interpretation or a different point of view. However, after spending considerable time in critically going through this work, I was disappointed, as the author has not been able to make a logical case for equating the Harappans with the Aryans. It was however nice to see B. Singh's well-produced book. The book is profusely illustrated, though frequently marred by errors of proof reading, grammar and syntax. He has really brought out a massive work, running into five hundred pages in an 8.5' x 11' format!

I must confess that I cannot pass any judgement on his linguistic interpretations of the Vedic literature as I have no competence in that field, nor do I know whether the author has. Not being a linguist, I would leave it to experts to comment on his linguistic capabilities and on the force of his linguistic arguments. I am thus reviewing it as an archaeologist, as the author has identified the Aryans with a known archaeological assemblage, i.e., the Harappa Culture. I will confine myself to the methodology and logic he has employed in this book. It would have been advisable for him to argue his case in a specialised linguistic journal so that the experts could critically examine it. I should concede that even though knowledge in a specialised field can never be the monopoly of a professional, a problem arises when a fiction writer tries to overturn current theories in the fields of both archaeology and linguistics, without any established expertise in either, notwithstanding his considerable strength in the use of invective and hyperbole. It requires a life-time of training in these technical disciplines to develop the insight and competence required to apply critically to such controversial issues.

The contrast becomes glaring when one compares, for example, the papers (in press) of R.S. Bisht, the famous excavator of Dholavira, and the well known historian Romila Thapar (1996) on the same theme. The rigour of logic and the capability of interpreting their evidence, besides their lucidity and coherence, are simply missing in *The Vedic Harappans.*

The main problem in Singh's book is that it starts with a very negative objective. Thus he has produced an eclectic assortment of data pulled out of context just to oppose the existing theories, which has resulted in an exercise in futility of an otherwise laudable effort. Instead, he would have made a more valuable contribution if he had confined himself to the reconstruction of the Vedic society, basing himself on the literary data. This could have given us a comprehensive picture of the material culture of the Aryans. Of course, he could also have compared the totality of the data and examined the merits of various Aryan equations *vis-a-vis* the known archaeological assemblages.

Some examples of his peculiar logic are as follows. Describing the Harappan society, he jumps to the conclusion, 'Certainly there was a guild with effective control' and then he crosses over to *Riv* (Rigveda) and brings in *purapati* and *Raja*, assuming that the Rigveda describes Harappan society. He reverses the movement of the Harappans from the Sarasvati to the Indus because of the drying up of the Sarasvati. In order to portray the Harappans as a merchant class he interprets *Rajas* as big merchants rather than as kings. His statements like, 'Rv itself refers to various types of government...', 'besides mention of the Rajnah ...which substantiates the hypothesis that there was no powerful empire through the length and the breadth of the Harappan civilisation,' leaves the reader totally confused about the difference between his assumptions and proof.

In Singh's book, assumptions and proofs mingle merrily all the time. Towards the later chapters, the author if nobody else, seems to be convinced of the Aryan = Harappan equation and gives up even the pretence of proving anything and freely uses the two as synonyms. Carried off by his own rhetoric he forgets that his main aim was to prove the equation of the Harappans with the Aryans!

In this light, his complaint that 'the histories written so far lack objectivity' sounds a bit farcical. He even thinks that Aryan technology was available not only to the Harappans but even to the pre-Harappans. This is one of the typical examples of his regard for archaeological evidence. If something goes against his assumptions, he simply discards it. When he is faced with the problem of the absence of horse in the Harappan context, he discards even the observations of well known zoo-archaeologists like Meadows and calls it 'aggressive American archaeology.' When confronted with the problem of the absence of the horse on the Harappan seals, he explains it away by saying that to be symbolised as God on seals 'an animal had to be unbridled... and ferocious.' Thus he makes even the poor goat look ferocious! He forgets that on page 421 of his own book, *Soma* is also deified as a horse but is not featured on Harappan seals. Similarly, *Maruts, Indra, Agni* and *Parjanya* are deified as lion in Rv, while the lion is significantly absent in Harappans seals. What could be more ferocious an animal the than lion, but he wriggles out of the problem by equating 'tiger[lion]', thus making them synonymous. Is this honest logic?

He easily explains away battles between the *Devas* and *Asuras*, as simply that between two opposite forces of human nature. This is also done when frequent references to war and destruction in the Rv are identified with differences in religious practices. Without adducing any evidence he calls the Aryans a peace loving people and that while the forts of the 'water-stealing demons' were allegorical those of the Aryans were real. To explain the epithet *anāsa* (snub nosed), he brings the Mongoloid Sakas into a third millennium context! At least Bisht is honest in accepting the evidence of the Aryan invasion and destruction of forts, although he believes that they also built their own forts. What Singh set out to prove, becomes itself a proof - another example of his confused logic. He says, 'what remains unexplained in the Rv gets clarified from the urban planning of the Harappans.'... An example of his unbridled imagination: 'This enclosure (at Dholavira) must have been for animals which were collected by way of tax and which could be given to charity or disposed of in the domestic or foreign market.' I wish the archaeologists too had a similar license to interpret their evidence or lack of it. Non-occurrence of any word for the potter in the Rv is easily explained away by him by identifying him with *Viśvarupa.* He asks, 'who was the mythical fabricator, if not a potter?' There is no limit to his fertile imagination: the evidence of broken shell bangles from the Harappan sites is interpreted as the continuance of the practice of widows' breaking their bangles at the death of their husband, which is a Vedic tradition! I wish somebody told him that most of the artefacts in archaeological sites are found in broken pieces, due to the pressure of the overlying accumulated debris and do not represent the grief of a widow!

More of his peculiar logic is as follows. He says, 'Harappans or the early Vedic artisans could not produce a high temperature as required for making glass and iron but it is they and their branch outside who were responsible for quality production of glass and iron.' (P.158) He even propounds that gold and silver currency were used by the Harappans (p.193)! He admits that although silver is not mentioned in the Rigveda, as they were acquainted with gold, they are bound to use silver too! '...In the face of terms like *chandrani* we are bound to admit to the existence of small chips of silver in currency.' One may perhaps ask as to where the evidence of such gold and silver chips of standard weight, which could be termed as currency, in the archaeological record. Further, he identifies *pavman soma* with smelting and processing of ores and minerals. He identifies *govid* with a 'good geologist' who could identify minerals (p. 218). No skeletons have been found at Dholavira, yet Singh has been able to determine the orientation of the head in graves. According to him the architecture of 'ordinary houses at the Harappan sites also confirms to Vedic descriptions.' He doesn't bother to amplify this point.

Only once in a while he admits that 'The most confounding thing about the Rv is that there is no mention of a city/country by name' (p. 253). But he wants us to believe that the Vedic *puras* were a stark reality while the *puras* of the Asuras were only allegorical descriptions of rain clouds, mineral-rich mountains, bands of pirates and robbers.

Singh doesn't seem to apply the same criteria to his own writing, though he himself is aware of the pseudo-scientific approach which consists of holding '*a priori assumptions*', and 'rejection of the unwanted results' and ending with equally 'fragile conclusions'... His Aryans automatically go back in antiquity as radiocarbon dates have pushed back the pre-Harappan cultures at Mehrgarh (Pakistan) to the seventh millennium BC! At one stage he seems to be admitting that 'The marauders disturbed the urban settlements... as far as the Indus,' but he reads in it only the disruption of the Harappan trade network. On the one hand, he thinks that the Aryans spread over the whole of Europe, and on the other, he talks of the ban on journeys outside the Aryan (territory) countries before the *Satpatha Brahman*.

Singh flatly denies the presence of female figures on Harappan seals, yet there are numerous examples of such figures be they goddesses or not. On page 402 he writes that 'schooling of a girl child was an aberration' and on page 403 that 'there was no bar on the education of females'. Such contradictions are abundant in his book. As goddesses do not fit into his patriarchal Aryan society, he dismisses the mother goddess terracottas as things made by children to play with. Is this not the limit of distortion! The juice of Soma extraction is compared to urine coming out of a penis and thus he explains the origin of phallus worship amongst the Harappans (p. 439). Let me quote one last example before I conclude. He explains as being the migration of people into India due to glaciations and their returning to northern latitudes due to climatic amelioration. Thus he forgets the theme of the global "Aryanising" mission of his Aryans and leaves them to the vagaries of climate.

From the above evaluation it becomes obvious that this book has been written only to prove that the Aryans originated in India and did not come from outside and is therefore a tendentious attempt and not a scientific analysis to arrive at truth. Genuine scholarship requires a more modest and constructive aim of reconstructing past material and non-material cultures critically using archaeological, literary and other data. One has to distinguish between myth-making and scientific writing.

Finally, as an archaeologist, believing in objective evidence, I would like to pose a few inconvenient questions to the protagonists of the Vedic Harappans. If the Harappans were indigenous Aryans, how do we explain the following points:

1. Unless there was a discontinuity, why was the Harappan script forgotten?

2. How is it, that in the II millennium BC after the pinnacle of planned urban towns of the Harappans there is an all round degeneration into non-urban cultures?

Of course, while people's belief systems and religion could not have been exterminated, even the brave Aryans could not have killed all the local people! And that explains the essentially non-Aryan substrate of Indian culture and religion. The rulers could be extirpated, their elite culture, polity, planning, script could be annihilated, but the culture at the people's level continues. In this connection it may be relevant to recall what I had written about this break in the polity (Agrawal 1993), "In the last quarter of the II millennium B.C., in the valley of Sarasvati, the population thins down drastically .... A bit later, iron starts appearing, so do the grey wares. Rice, pig and buffalo become prominent in the subsistence record. In the Chalcolithic cultures, lentils and leguminous plants appear and assume importance in the diet, they were conspicuous by their absence in the Harappan record. The literate tradition breaks, no script any more. Use of ground water and wells is given up, along with the burnt bricks. No more planned towns, in fact, no more towns. The ones that were there lose their character and population. It does not mean that populations were decimated, but with lack of control from the metropolitan centres, the provincial towns degenerated and changed....For the first time the *lota* and *thali* are introduced in the Indian crockery by the Kayatha culture and continue to this day. Now burials come right into the houses: the dead of the Chalcolithic cultures are buried below the house floors, unlike the Harappan cemeteries located outside settlements....These markers, in diet, in subsistence, in script and literate tradition, in daily items of use, which suddenly disappeared after the Harappans, are obviously conveying the message that the cultural tradition broke down. To my mind, it signifies the advent of a new people who were now the new rulers and dictated new fashions. The break of tradition is writ large on the evidence."

It will be pertinent to quote here from *Earth Mother* written by Pupul Jaykar who spent a life time in the study of folklore, folk culture, myths and legends. "In the frantic escape from the waves of storming invaders, in the following centuries of persistent pressure, much that was identifiable in the Harappan culture disappeared. The vast storehouses of art and technology, magic and ritual, merged into the surrounding agricultural societies or reappeared transformed in the icons and artefacts of the dwellers along the river valleys, on the Deccan plateau, or in the faces of the *Grama Devatas* of the autochthons of the south." Further, she says, "Janapadas led to a surface disappearance of ancient mother rights amongst vast masses of the population, but an archaic people's culture based on the primacy of the female principle survived in secret women's rites and fertility rituals. The Aryan invaders, who sought to destroy this ancient culture, were instead, assimilated."

All this is not to deny the legacy of the Harappans to the mosaic of the Indian Culture. India was invaded by innumerable hordes of people, the British, the Huns, the Greeks, the Aryans, the Muslims and so on, but the basic stream of the Indian culture continued to flow, and all these minor tributaries commingled with the main river through time. In fact, the Harappa culture provided its oldest substratum, as I have stated elsewhere, "The (Hindu) religion is basically iconic and not animistic as that of the Aryans. The *pasupata, yogisvara, trimukha* aspects of the famous seals have been identified as proto-Siva, or even proto-Mahisa.... and to me it appears to be a strong evidence. The Nandi bull worship has to be traced to the Harappans, and perhaps the sacredness of the cow too. Some of the seals suggest animal sacrifice, so does the terracotta cake from Kalibangam ... the Linga worship can only be traced to the Harappans, even if the phallus like objects are few and some scholars do not believe that the proto-Siva seal shows an ithyphallic god. The importance of pipal (*Ficus religiosa*) swastika, and water ablution in today's religion can be traced back to the Harappan preoccupation with water rituals (e.g., the Great Bath, the associated water structures with the Kalibangan fire altars, the row of bathing platforms at Lothal etc.) and the emphasis on the pipal motif do suggest a continuity of the religious beliefs. The enigmatic terracotta figures do suggest yoga like postures.... Even secular objects like the typical Harappan house plan of a central courtyard surrounded by rooms (it has been found by air-conditioning experts to be best suited for Indian climate) seems to have continued from the Harappan times. The binary system of weight of the Harappans followed 1,2,4,8,16,32,64,.....12800, with fractions in one-third. Till recently, the Indian 1 seer = 16 chattacks and 1 rupee = 16 annas basically followed the same system. Even the Arthasastra's *angula* of 17.86 millimetres seems to have been derived from the Harappan measuring unit of 17.7 millimetres. What the present Indian culture owes to the Indus Civilisation will perhaps never be known fully as the intangible heritage that we got from the Harappans can never be fully traced to its Harappan origins, unless one day one finds long decipherable texts of the Harappans...' (Agrawal, op. cit.)

To quote Jaykar again, "Two movements emerged out of the fusion of the Aryans and the autochthons: the Vedic or *margi* directed to ritual, incantations and sacrifice, intended to propitiate the gods, and the non-Vedic or *desi* propelled by magic and alchemy, concerned with Vrata and Tantric ritual, acts to control and change the course of things. Further, "The Atharva Veda, compiled by singing sages several centuries after the Rgvedic hymns, contains very archaic elements and is possibly the earliest record of the beliefs, the imagery, the rituals and worships of the autochthonous people of India as they met and transformed the conquering Aryan consciousness."

To sum up, we need more solid and logical arguments, than one finds in the Vedic Harappans, to give away the great Harappa Culture on a platter to the Aryans alone.

REFERENCES

Agrawal, D.P. 1993. Ecological Factors and the Harappan Civilisation in *Harappan Civilization. A Recent Perspective,* (G.L. Possehl Ed.), pp 223-233. American Institute of Indian Studies and Oxford amp&; IBH publishing Co. Pvt. Ltd.

Thapar, Romila 1996. The Theory of Aryan Race and Indian History and Politics, *Social Scientist,* 24 (1-3).

D. P. Agrawal

Reply to **Dr. D.P. Agrawal's,** Review of the book *The Vedic Harappans* by Bhagwan Singh.

Marxist historiography is passing through serious strains, not because it has lost its relevance, but because a number of historians claiming Marxist credentials have undermined the basic tenets of dialectical materialism. They resort to shortcuts and spread canards on some pretext or the other, making at times irresponsible statements. The malady is old, but it had never reached its critical point as in recent years. As a case I intend to examine a review of *The Vedic Harappans* by Dr. D.P.Agrawal especially because it invites a reply.

It was just a chance that I came across a review of the *Vedic Harappans* by D.P.Agrawal on the Internet. Three years back when he informed me of having devoted one month's time to reading it, I was really pleased. He had to borrow the book from a library, as neither the publisher, nor the author, nor any journal had sent the book to him for review. He had shown an extraordinary gesture.

Dr. Agrawal is a scientist by education, an archaeologist by training, a teacher by profession and a Marxist by affiliation. In weak moments of vainglory, he may inform that he has published 150, may be more, articles in international journals, which speaks enough for his stature. A work on which a scholar like him had devoted one month's time could not be wished away. I was, therefore, thankful for his unasked generosity.

Had he not raised two questions to be answered by the author, it would have been better to ignore the review, which, true to his proclivity, tells little about the book and much about the reviewer. Moreover, it raises some questions about the dubious contribution of 'Marxist' school in promotion or escalation of Indian learning in the field of social sciences. Among the Indian Marxists, some are Marxists and some are more Marxists, while others are simply leftists:

"Accusations of being a Menshevic or a Bolshevik, of being reactionary or a progressive, could be hurled from a 'boxwallah' to an independent ... without a shadow of guilt or absurdity. ... It was to take me many years to discover that even the fire-blowing revolutionary was suddenly stunted when confronted with the white man or with authority in general. ...We were still blissfully unaware of the steep divisions which separated party members from the outside world as well as from each other." (Raj Thapar, *All These Years,* Penguin India, 1991, pp. 6,9, 28).

2.

Agrawal starts with a search of soft spots. He tries the Hindutva tag only to concede that it does not stick.

Ultimately, he informs his readers that the author is a creative writer. He grunts that the book is well illustrated and elegantly produced. He mocks the author for syntactical, grammatical and proof mistakes in the book but does not point out even a single one. He admits that he is incompetent to judge the literary and linguistic merit of the book and sends a suppressed whimper that the author himself might not be competent on those aspects. He promises to confine himself within the area of his expertise but as easily forgets his promise and mostly raises points pertaining to language and literature with expected naivete. Only thrice he raises objections on archaeological grounds and quotes himself elaborately to answer everything. Out of the three, in one case he is definitely correct - subsequent excavations have proved the guess of this author wrong. The other is distortion and the last one an alternative suggestion.

In his enthusiasm to overkill he does not find anything positive in the book. As he has pointed out only the shortcomings and nothing else, it may be surmised that barring the three errors he could not detect any archaeological flaw in the book, and, as we have pointed out, at least in one case he is correct. Had I been proved wrong on all the three scores, even that would not have made any substantial change in our position as they are all of marginal value. The rest of the points fall outside his area of competence and therefore humbug. The beauty is that he bares his teeth more often than he bares his arguments.

He objects to the methodology adopted in the book, but the methodology adopted by him is disgusting. He quotes the author in fragments, mostly without mentioning the page number. He is found distorting, mutilating, dilating and misquoting the views of the author to make him vulnerable. If this be the ideal methodology, one may better leave it for him to follow.

3

I do not claim to be in ideal command of English. In fact, I have no command on any language except Hindi, my mother tongue, and have only working knowledge of a few others, including English. Indian Marxists have greater regard for chaste English as it sets the masses apart from the masters:

"Many of the bright boys of the Communist Party of India came from powerful families, for only they could think of sending their children abroad for education; they were bolshevised in England because that was the reigning intellectual trend, a direct result of fascism and the second world war" (*op. cit.*, p.8).

Love of king's English, besides other colonial biases, is infused in Indian Marxist thinking. No sensible scholar turns to academic works to improve his grammar. If the idea is communicated the language and grammar can wait for perfection. The demand for linguistic perfection narrows the area of participation and is, therefore, academically counterproductive.

Dr. Agrawal habitually cooks to conquer. Barring one or two exceptions, he cites my views from the conclusive remarks, imputing notions contrary to my views. He picked up '*equid*' not from the chapter on horse, but the chapter on mythology and religion. He picks up a term from the 'Index', namely '*govid*' (geologist) but does not take the trouble of checking the text to see what forms the basis of that observation. He hides from his readers the fact that I have used 'currency' in a limited sense as evident from inverted commas. I have defined the term in the text. He jeers that I talk of gold and silver currency in Harappan context. Deliberate mutilations and distortions have become the hallmark of overactive leftist harangues so he is not alone to blame. Dr. Shereen Ratnagar is reported (HT, 18.8.2000) to have informed her audience that "Even in the Rigveda, there is only one reference to the Saraswati river as the river of rivers." According to her those who claimed that Aryans were an indigenous people, belong to the left wing and the claim is false. She is stated to have alleged, "Unless they do this, they cannot forward the logic that certain minorities owe their existence in this country to invasions. If they concede that Aryans were also migrants to this country, then they will have to apply the same yardstick to themselves." Disputations arising out of imputations, patent lies and wild imagination do not show a good sense of history. The learned Professor is either totally blank on the Vedic side or is not forthright in her remarks. She should have consulted the Index of the Ṛgveda or the *Vedic Index of Names and Subjects* to know that Sarasvati is mentioned more than 70 times in the Ṛgveda. It is the only river that is deified in the Ṛgveda. The only one to be invoked with other deities. The only river mentioned prominently in five hymns (1.3.10-12, 2.16-18; 6.61; 7.96.4-6). The only one whose valley is said to be peopled by the *pañca janãh* (whatever it may mean). Ignorance is certainly a bliss, but such a total collapse of academic culture is lamentable. We wonder the amount of freedom granted to and enjoyed by demented left-wing scholars. Is it Marxism? Does secularism permit constant enticement to minority phobia? In any case, Agrawal has a wide support base.

He writes, "I should concede that a specilised field can never be the monopoly of a professional, a problem arises when a fiction writer tries to overturn current theories in the field of both archaeology and linguistics." The dust-cover mentions our work on linguistics published in early seventies. He picked up fiction and unread the rest. Agrawal conceals the real problem. In his formative days, he found it beneficial to join the chorus of the Aryan invasion of India. It endeared him to the cultural imperialists abroad and the scholars controlling social sciences at home, who fought 'revivalism' with colonial tools. *The Vedic Harappans,* with its massive data and clinching evidence, demolished that theory down to its foundations. He knows that it can not be upheld any more and feels perturbed.

On my part, neither do I claim to have changed any theory in archaeology, nor in linguistics. I totally rely on data and competent authorities, but not the outdated ones. I rarely offer my surmises except in the blank spaces, in-between. It is for Agrawal and the like of him to explain why, being professionals, they still talk of Aryan invasion of India, whereas archaeology assailed it four decades back. It is for them to tell which crucial linguistic evidence is available to prove the emergence of Indo-European outside India? The alarm, 'save linguistics from the fiction writer' is faulted. He appears to be ignorant of the fact that linguistics is a chimerical discipline changing hues according to the areas, expertise and national prejudices.

"... there are as many different approaches to its study as there are to knowledge in general. The humanist, the social scientist, and the natural scientist each has a stake in understanding how language works; each branch of scholarship approaches language with its particular set of assumptions and methodologies, and focuses on that aspect most germane to its central concerns" (Frederick J. Newmeyer, *The Politics of Linguistics,* 1986, p.4).

Agrawal appears to be ignorant of even the basics of linguistics and is still tempted to pass remarks on the competence of one who had published two works of linguistics.

He taunts me for being a creative writer, which I claim to be my forte. He is unaware that fiction writers have in a number of cases foreshadowed the future inventions and discoveries and even Jayant Narlikar writes fiction to keep his sensitivities alive. Stuffed brains, having no literary training, and lacking in imagination like stone, could not write the history of a period entirely based on a superb literary work, having layers and layers of meaning. Look at the discomfiture of such scholars: (a) They count the occurrence of *go,* cattle, to prove that the Vedic subsistence was primarily pastoral. They merrily ignore that the term occurs for earth, water, dawn, speech, sense organs, milk, butter, skin and many other things beside cattle. Bad statistics indeed! (b) They fail even to connect the cattle breeding with archaeological records, as cattle breeding has been practised in the subcontinent from the Mehargarh down to the present times on a scale much bigger than the neighbouring countries. (c) They fail to connect it with cultural anthropology. Herding in India has always been cattle intensive while in the neighbouring countries it has been sheep/goat oriented. It is Krishna who is called cowboy, not Jesus who is the shepherd of his 'flock'. (d) They fail to reach deeper layers of the allegories, ironies, puns, subtle connotations, and allusions, which make the text somewhat impermeable. (e) They even fail to make distinction between written text and oral literature, although the specimens are there, in the form of Vedic and *Purāṇic* texts. The former could not be composed without the help of written signs, the latter shows little that makes the use of written symbols imperative. It is precisely in these areas that I contributed a little that made the big difference.

It must be pointed out that Vedic problem is not a linguistic problem but a literary one. Even if one considers the problem to be essentially linguistic, he should equip himself as a linguist before passing judgement on competence of someone having published works to his credit.

An honest reviewer is expected to introduce the book first and to make observations later. He is a bridge between the book and the readers. A line from the dust cover could have done a bit of justice: "Massive data elucidating most, if not all, aspects of Harappan material culture including agriculture, industry, mining and metallurgy, trade, navigation, language, social set up, urban planning, public administration and religious belief make it immensely valuable...." Any disparagement after this brief introduction could be justified. But then he could not distort the way he distorted. It is simply recalcitrant to pick isolated words from the book to be reviewed and to cite para after para from other works to make the review wholesome. I feel obliged to help the readers. The book is divided into fourteen chapters. In the initial chapters: Preliminary observations; The myth of Aryan invasion; The horse and the Aryans; and Nature of the Vedic conflicts, we examine and cancel the prevailing views on the Aryan invasion and dichotomy between Harappan civilisation and Aryan culture. In the process it is established that Ṛgveda is a Harappan text and Harappan material culture is inalienably Vedic. Now it proceeds to examine the aspects of civilisation: Stock breeding and agriculture; Harappan pottery in the Ṛgveda; industry; Mineral resources of Vedic merchants; Navigation; Overland trade and commerce; Housing and urban centres; The language the Harappans spoke; The social mosaic; and Mythology and religion, followed by Bibliography and Index. Each chapter is divided into sections, the first one presents, as objectively as possible, the prevailing opinion, the circumstances under which this opinion was formed and ensuing omissions and commissions. In the following sections it embarks upon a detailed discussion of Harappan material and Ṛgvedic accounts, comparing, complementing and reinforcing the views from both the sources. The final section subtitled 'Conclusion' is a gist of discussions, which on an average is one page in length, or the 1/30 of the body text. I think it to be quite fair, unless some one claims that the citations are flawed, interpretations untenable, or some author has been misquoted. Even in his diabolical review Agrawal has not charged me of deliberate failing on these accounts. The old method had been that of presenting one-sided view, ignoring inconvenient views, and castigating those who raised questions. It still continues in many universities. Even students asking questions in higher classes were and are still harassed either to change their subject or to discontinue their research. Highly biased views foreshadowing academic disaster were presented in selfsame-manner, which were not only presumptive, but, quite often, self-defeating. Marxism struggled to survive through other means, controlling minds, stifling researches and discouraging new ideas. Indian Marxists do not allow their adversaries to demolish them, they do the job themselves. One is reminded of the old orthodox Hindus who did perform their last rites before proceeding on pilgrimage in olden days. These are happy occasions where orthodox Hinduism and 'revolutionary' Marxism embrace each other.

Agrawal alleges that I have "produced eclectic assortment of data pulled out of context to oppose the existing theories." It is simply a self-projection. Elaborate, if not, exhaustive data, citations from all possible angles are neatly marshalled to prove a point. If multilateral approach has limitations, it has many plus points that compensate the loss. But as already pointed out Agrawal resorts to tricks to berate the book. He offers "some examples of" our peculiar logic: "'Certainly there was a guild with effective control' and then he crosses over to Ṛgveda and brings in *purapati* and *Rājā* assuming that the Ṛgveda describes the Harappan society. He reverses the movement of the Harappans from Sarasvati to Indus because of the drying up of the Sarasvati. In order to portray Harappans as a big merchant class he interprets Rajas as big merchants than as kings...His statements like, 'Rv itself refers to various types of government...', 'besides mention of the Rājanaḥ ...which substantiates the hypothesis that there was no powerful empire through the length and the breadth of the Harappan civilisation,' leave the reader totally confused between his assumption and the proof." Note that there are three fragmentary quotes interspersed with the *'gist'* of author's views in reviewer's words, but no page number is given in any case. The reader has to believe the reviewer, because he can not check the veracity of the allegations. I myself failed to locate some of them. I remember to have used guild in the sense of *śreṇī*. I could not assume the Harappan society to be composed of 'big businessmen.' I hold that big business men were present in Harappan society. Mineral exploitation from distant lands, overseas trade, advance planning of the cities built on raised platforms, presuppose existence of big traders in Harappan society, and an institution like guild of historical periods. Likewise I have placed my arguments as to why all the notable personalities, mentioned in the RV, need not be taken for kings. The term *rājā*, meaning the illustrious one, was used for the heads of big business houses. *Rājā* Amichand, *rājā* Shivaprasad from recent history could be forgotten, but the fact that Agrawal forgets his own lineage from rājā Agrasena, is funny. I refer to the existence of a rich merchant class in the RV and occurrence of the term *śreṇī*. The term occurs on page 265 with elaborate textual material, *rājā* on 271, 314 etc. with sufficient justification, while *purpati* occurs on page 312, in a list of technical terms, and in conclusive remarks on page 319. He meshes all into one chain to invent a shortcoming.

I have dwelt on horse in a separate chapter to prove that the term aśva earlier signified ass. Synonyms of ass were transferred to horse. Horse was not found in plenty during the Mature Harappan period, but ass was. I gave my explanation why horse was not depicted on the seals, "... we are faced with another problem, namely why did they not find horse adorable enough to be depicted on seals. But once we realise that Harappan seal-motifs represent the deities, the haze is dispelled. In the Ṛgveda, *Agni, Indra, Soma, Rudra, Brahmanaspati,* etc. have been personified as goat, bull, boar, lion (tiger), elephant, buffalo, eagle, etc. To be symbolised as a god, an animal had to be unbridled, intractable and ferocious. It is not just a coincidence that almost all the animals depicted on seals are fierce looking? Even the goat is not an exception. It is also not a chance that they are all male. It is also not a chance that the mother goddesses, not considered worthy of seal motifs, are awe inspiring in their models. Only the powerful could protect (p.72)." Agrawal does not mention the page number, but builds tripartite logic on this score. (1) He points to a citation in the chapter on mythology and religion, page 421, where, in a verse *aśva* occurs in the context of Soma, to prove me wrong. (2) He alleges that I deliberately equate lion with tiger and (3) that I deny the presence of female figures on Harappan seals. He distributes these remarks so as no one could detect the exact location.

The citation on page 421 refers to ass, not horse. The term used is *kradat,* brays. The simile refers to the sound produced by the oil-pressure like instrument applied for extracting Soma juice. The real epithet is that of lion, *aśvo na krado vṛṣabhir yujānah sinho na bhimo manaso javīyān,* that is, braying like an ass, fearsome like a lion, moving at will, harnessed by bulls (those who extract the juice). Harappan material yields ass bones in abundance, but I do not recollect an ass to have been depicted on a seal. Why? I have mentioned the reason.

It is not my invention, that *sinha* covers both lion and tiger. It is Yask who was not answering the inventive scholarship. He says *sinho vyāghra iti pujāyam* (nir. 3.18) in adulation lion is tiger. The Vedic references are adulatory in nature. Large number of seals admittedly, served votary purposes.

He distorts my statement when he says, "Singh flatly denies the presence of female figures on Harappan seals. I have said that female animal figures are not present on seals" (*supra*), i.e. all types of bulls but no cow, Male unicorn but no female unicorn, male goat but no she goat and so on. In fact even mother goddesses are absent on seals while Rudra is there. How enigmatic is it for a society advocated to be matriarchal! I have elaborately discussed the fertility cult (p.426-28), citing relevant portions from the text. I have shown perfect correspondence between the famous seal with upturned, outstretched legs, a plant growing from her vestibule, and a Vedic verse describing exactly the same.

Agrawal makes light of my suggestion that '*govid*' could, among other things, signify 'a geologist, i.e. a judge of mineral rich rocks and the merits and demerits of stones. He picks this word from the 'index' and jumps to subjective inferences. He either did not check the relevant pages 217-218, where it is argued on merit, or deliberately resorted to half-truth as evident from non-mention of the pages in the text. He knows only one meaning of *go*, i.e. cattle; only one meaning of *gopa*, i.e. cow boy, only one meaning of professionalism, i.e. not to admit anything that demolishes your thesis. We may remind that cows of Indra are the gems known as *indra-nīla-maṇi*, or *nīlam*, sapphire and turqoise while *gomed* signified stones with other hues.

He ignores the multilateral evidence to support that the Aryans were peace-loving people. He has again taken fragments from conclusive section, chapter VI. Even so, he neither quotes me, nor gives the page number, for obvious reasons. I quote from this very section, "In retrospect, we may submit that the Aryans were not 'a wild, turbulent people" (Basham 1953,37) as they have been made out to be. They loved peace around and calm within. Their poetry depicting the cosmic drama was either misunderstood or misinterpreted to build the image of war loving Aryans. The *purs* of water-stealing demons were allegorical while those of the 'Aryans' were real. In the discussion part, among other things, I have cited 21 verses in Griffith's translation to show that they disliked confrontation with enemies. There is a complete section on their sense of insecurity, a statistical analysis of the words signifying victory, insecurity, cry for protection or non-confrontation with their enemies. There are a large number of verses with the theme *śāntipāṭha* starting with '*śam*' and again there are a number of *swastipāṭhas*. There are clear statements that all the accounts of Indra's wars are allegorical - Indra neither fought anyone nor conquered any. There is much more besides, given in detail and yet he cunningly misinforms his readers that "without adducing any evidence he calls the Aryans a peace loving people".

Agrawal says that I "admit that silver is not mentioned in the RV". This is simply a travesty of the truth. What I have written is this: "It has been suggested that silver is conspicuous by its absence or relative absence in the Ṛgveda (Macdonnel, 1908, 221) whereas it was more commonly used in all forms in the 'Indus society' (Marshall, 1931, 110). This notion has acquired an unassailable sanctity, because no one pointed out that besides *rajata* which occurs only once (VIII.25.22), there is yet another term for silver in the Ṛgveda, namely, *candra> cāndī*, the most popular of our terms for silver, which tells a lot by its occurrence in various forms. After this I have referred to 39 verses (p.185). I have drawn six parallel citations (p.193, fn.) between *hiraṇya* and *chandra*, i.e., *hiraṇya ratah / chandra ratha; hiraṇya varṇa /chandra varṇa; hiraṇyani / chandraṇ nirṇik / chandra nirṇik; hiraṇyamiva / chandramiva*; the sixth one being a prayer addressed to soma that he may fill the poets/clients house with *candra* and *hiraṇya*.

Agrawal blatantly misquotes me, he says, "Harappans or the early Vedic artisans could not produce a high temperature as required for making glass and iron but it is they and their branch outside, who were responsible for quality production of glass and iron. Here again he has picked up a fragment from the Conclusion' section of chapter VI (p.158). Why was he so parsimonious as to leave only the two words that made all the difference? The last segment even in my summary statement is "quality production of *steatite, stoneware, glass and iron.*" In the text section I have quoted authorities Dales and Mackay and referred to Tel-el-Amerna (138-40).

In racial Euro-centric explanation *anās* means snub-nosed which is inconsistent with traditional explanation 'mouthless', more rationally explained as mute, *bejabān*, or *vadhṛivāc*. There is only one occurrence of this overused term. I have thrown one suggestion with reference to Ana-sa-na in view of the vast area in which they were active.

I have used *'currency'* within inverted commas. I have explained "It must be conceded that currency may not be the proper term for the chips of gold, silver and copper as they are likely to be used as stuff rather than coins of defined values." He is dishonest in presenting my thesis. As a professional, he must know that in old civilisations weight and purity of chips of gold and silver was checked at every transaction, and at the appropriate level goods were exchanged for the chips of precious metals. Metal by its very nature, had to be available in pieces of different denominations to be conveniently handed over to the customers.

I have no where asserted that skeletons were found at Dholavira. I made my judgement on the basis of exposed pits with burial pottery. That is sufficient for judging the angular irregularities in orientation of the pits. I have not referred to orientation as a supportive evidence but as an aberration, "somewhat inconsistent with traditional orientation."

He again distorts my statement, "He easily explains away battles between the Deva and Asuras, as simply that between two opposite forces of human nature." No page mentioned. I have discussed it in a section (p.79-84), specifying its various shades which may be obvious even in fragmentary quotes, "two clear divisions and subdivisions in the Vedic society..."(p.79). "... the terms related to subsistence pattern to show that they (Devas) had made some such progress in production technique as left (to have left) their enemies far behind..." (p.81). "Serious differences over religious practices..." (p.81). But the most important aspect of the Deva-Asura tangle is that it could have gathered a new dimension in the course of Harappan trade..." (81-82).

I have explained why I consider the *asura purs* as ethereal and the Vedic ones to be real. They are also called "*cariṣṇu*, mobile, *manojava*, moving at minds speed. Ninety nine of them are said to have been smashed with one stroke, they are torn like tattered cloth and gored as if by horn. Those of the Aryans are *āyasī adhṛṣtā*, metal like strong and invincible. But how can I convince a man who is fond of jumping into areas of his ignorance and talking lose confessing that he knows little.

Agrawal derides my suggestion that the mythical fabricator, *viśvarūpā*, may be divine potter, as "this is the limit of fertile imagination". He forgets his pathological lack of imagination when he makes us believe that a society using a large range of utensils, 37 types of them are listed by me on (p.154-56), imported its pottery, or perhaps grew the pottery as grass. The central point is not whether *viśvarūpa* is a divine potter or not, the point is whether such a range of pottery could be made without professional potters and could be managed by nomadic herders? Notorious 'professionalism' made us believe that Aryans had language but no archaeology.

Agrawal quotes himself extensively to restate the fossilised old view that "The Hindu religion is basically iconic and not animistic as that of Aryans..." He appears not to have seen the chapter on mythology and religion, in which these notions are examined. If he had really read he should have criticised me instead of quoting himself. However, if cow worship is Harappan, Harappan for him means non-Aryan, that is non Vedic, then how did the concept of the sacredness of cow reach the Parsis, why in Zend Avesta cow is called *agnya*, (Vedic *aghnya*), and why even its urine is held sacred? If Aryan religion is animistic, how do the so called Mundari tribes practice animism? If *pīpala* is non-Aryan why *aśvattha* is said to be the abode of the Vedic deities. If binary system is non-Aryan, how come the bargaining in case of Soma-purchase takes place in binary system. Has he any justification for the use of *kalā* i.e. 1/16th and *śafa* i.e. 1/8th in RV? If *swastic* is non Aryan, why does is occur only in the Vedic texts and tradition. In fact every point mentioned by Agrawal in his extensive self-quotation, shows his pathetic lack of knowledge and understanding.

He quotes Pupul Jaykar to evince that Aryan invasion of India is a reality, "In the frantic escape from the waves of storming invaders..." No professional scholar takes shelter behind a non-professional. Jaykar's readings of folklore are apparently diluted. The lore and legends speak of *asuras*, not the *devas*, as aggressors, haughty, more powerful, numerically superior, *raktavījas*, living in forests, practising hunting and gathering and ignorant of civilised norms. The two are always shown as half-brothers, one on the side of the dark and the other on the side of light, in every respect. In the lore of pastoral societies, the Indra worshipers are agriculturist. On the one hand there is Govind, Gopāla, the cowboy, and *govardhana*, promotion of cattle breeding, on the other we have Sankarsana, Baladeva, Halayudha, tiller, peasant, and *indramaha* or sacrifice for rain. Yet both are half brothers, complementary to each other.

Rudra and mother godesses, and *yoga*, are as much Harappan as Vedic. The mother goddess is not a deity of habitations. She is *aranyānī, durgā, pārvatī*, moving in forests and hills. Her platform was erected outside the village preferably under a *nīma* tree, which symbolised the forest. Her epithets, *chāmundā, kālikā, kapālakuṇḍalā*, are reminiscent of cannibalism. So is the case with Lord Shiva, retaining his seniority as a deity, *mahādeva, mahendra, devānām jyeṣtha* and *śreṣtha* who is also *kapālī*, and the god of destruction, *rudra, bhairava*. Their cults are *tantra*, permissive of human sacrifice and *haṭhayoga*, extreme form of austerity practised in secluded places. They were worshipped in some areas in Harappan society but not universally. That is what I have elaborately discussed in the light of literary evidence as well. Dr. Agrawal has a disturbed conscience and a perturbed mind not to be able to understand it.

As far as the pressure on herders and gatherers is concerned, it must be acceded that there has been continuous pressure from the peasants who converted grasslands into cornfields and further enlarged their estates by burning woodlands. They definitely deprived the gatherer-hunter communities of their source of sustenance, and exerted limited pressure on herders. The former were forced to recede back under pressure. The process continues till this day. The resistance of forest dwellers in those days was far stronger than it is today. That part of the folklore is part of real history. It is also supported by Puranic accounts in which, devas acquire new lands deceitfully and occasionally face the onslaughts of the agonised gatherers.

4

Agrawal poses two questions:

1. Unless there was a dichotomy, why was the Harappan script forgotten?

2. How is it, that in the II millennium BC after the pinnacle of planned urban towns of the Harappans there is an all round degeneration into non-urban cultures?

I advise him to read the second part of my book, *Harappā Sabhyatā aur Vaidik Sāhitya* (1987). *The Vedic Harappans* covers only the first part of that book.

For his convenience I may point out that invasions do not cause discontinuity; catastrophes and upheavals certainly do. Agrawal has himself mentioned many invasions of India. It is for him to answer which one caused discontinuity? It was protracted drought and famine interspersed with erratic rain and floods and the anarchy prevailing during that period in which people fought for survival. It was this experience that generated the idea of *yugsandhi*, or a very long period of darkness. Interlocking of late Harappan ware, handmade course gray and deluxe painted gray ware in archaeological record have preserved the gory tale of bloody fights and counter fights the exact gravity of which is still obscure. It has to be studied in adequate depth. The drought and famine have been mentioned in *Śatapatha Brāhmaṇa,* recounted in *Mahābhārat* and corroborated archaeologically from Central Asia to South Asia. It was during this period that the inhabitable marshlands across Sadānīrā, got dry and were populated by the refugees from Sarasvati Valley. Even so, writing was not completely discarded. It was not used for the purposes of trade and commerce and administration as the entire region underwent sever climatic stress which ruined the trade network, and various other urban forms, including craft, industry, transportation, cultural activities and smooth governance. In order to survive, they en-masse reverted to agriculture and cattle breeding and settled precariously close to water sources.

I have better explanation for introduction of a few new features mentioned by Agrawal and others. This calamitous time forced the a number of Harappans settled in northern Afghanistan, northern Iran and Central Asia, the entire Bactria Margiana Complex, or Uttara Kuru of Puranas, to fall back on their motherland in their distress. These traders settled abroad were in constant touch with their home country. It is evident from Harappan trade pattern, Harappan settlements, Ṛgvedic allusions and Puranic accounts. Comparison may be made with the Indians doing their business for centuries in Afghanistan who had to migrate to India because of the Taliban. As noted by many scholars, and never contradicted by any, the Harappans, and as admitted by Masson, the Aryans, formed the oligarchy there. Their gradual desertion brought about the doom of the urban and proto-urban sites: "At almost the same time in north-eastern Iran, Tepe Hissar and Turang tepe were depopulated, and the same thing happened on the plain of adjoining Kopet Dag range in two local centers - Namazga-depe and Altyn-depe" (V.M.Masson, in *The Dawn of Civilization: earliest times to 700 BC.* Unesco, ed. Dani and Masson, 1992). If presence of horse is slightly more pronounced during this period, so it must be. What else could carry their children and belongings back home?

Enough explanations have been sought from those rejecting the Aryan invasion theory. Almost all of them have been raised and answered by me in my book. It is now the turn of the supporters of the Aryan invasion of India or migration into India to explain:

1. Why did the Vedic society live in constant fear of the enemies, especially when moving in sizeable groups?

2. Why there is recurrent mention ot navigation in the Ṛgveda?

3. How does peacock occur in Harappan, Ṛgvedic, Elamite, Assyrian and Mitanni arts/text?

4. Why the cars and wagons are mentioned in the RV as loaded with goods?

5. Which part of Central Asia is known for cattle herding and from which Aryan pastorals came with their bovine culture?

6. Why are there only exceptional references to grazing in the Ṛgveda?

7. Why is the source of 'horse' said to be the 'Sea' or 'Water', not even once a steppe right from the Veda to the Puranic accounts?

8. Why are only the Aśvins, not known for chivalry, shown coming with the 'chariots'? Why are they

always expected to come with precious goods of all sorts, but not with soldiers? Why do they invariably occur in dual?

9. Why do the anthropologists concede that there was no influx of new people on a tangible scale right from 4500 BC down to 8th century BC or still later, while the 'professional Marxists' sing the old song of waves of invaders *ad nauseam*? Why there is no evidence of attack on Harappan cities or habitations? Why the desertion of Harappan and Late Harappan sites is not sudden but slow and steady?

10. Why is there no mention of war weapons - bow and arrows - in allusions to 'killings' of black forces? Why is this act repeated daily with the rise of the Moon and the Sun? How even 'Dawn' could be the annihilator of the black forces and even Indra crusher of dawn's chariot?

11. Why is Sarasvati a mighty and perennial river in the Veda while it had almost dried during Late Harappan and Post Harappan periods? Mind it, there is no proof of incoming Aryans but hard proof of people moving to Afghanistan, Iran and central Asia from Indus-Sarasvati region. Austerity demands of a scholar to rely on hard facts rather than conjectures.

12. Why is Shambara said to be dwelling in hilly terrain and Vrtra in the water bodies and clouds? Why even later Yaksas are said to be keeping guard on water bodies and not allowing anyone to drink without their permission.

13. Why have all sorts of roads, said to be reaching the farthest lands, been mentioned in the Ṛgveda and why is their movement through roads, rather than grasslands.

14. Why do the Vedic householders keep waiting for those gone out and express concern about their safety? Why are they supposed to cross many rivers - Kubha, Krumu, Anitabha, and Sindhu - on their homeward journey?

15. Why are there exactly the same devices of safeguarding their precious items both in Harappan cities and the Vedic references?

16. Why are there the same tools? Why the same dresses and ornaments? Why the same cattle wealth? Why the same Halls, the same Baths, the same multi-storey buildings in notable contexts, the same channels, the same collection pits, the same wells, the same cultic plants, the same account of mixed population, the same cage, the same tamed birds?

17. Why did old Iranians and even Greeks, especially Spartans, dress in the same way as the Harappans and the Vedic?

18. Why have over active historians not been able to archaeologically connect any culture with the 'Aryans'? A people with more than thirty seven types of utensils, a range of ornaments, weapons, tools, dwellings, hairstyles, dresses, cosmetics, is archeologically missing because of professionals like Dr. Agrawal. Why do the supporters of Aryan invasion jump so thoughtlessly on anything and try to hold fast even to floating straws coming their way?

19. How did the language of the cattle-breeders reach the Classical height and became as perfect, if not more, as the languages at the peak stage of civilisations, such as Greek, Latin, Arabic and Persian? How is Vedic replete with technical terms covering the entire gamut of Harappan achievements? Has a language any relation with the social, economic, technological and cultural realities or does it develop in a vacuum created by hollow minds?

20. Why is our 'leftist' approach racist, aggressive, irrational and fed on scandals and half-truths, in short, why is it fascist? Why despite all the researches it keeps repeating Grandma's gossips,

as if nothing changes in and around it? What purpose does it serve by the refrain that India was invaded time and again by foreigners? Which country is an exception? England suffered many more invasions within a short period of its history than India through its history of five thousand years. But that does not mean that a conjectural invasion of Aryans be entertained to sustain the credibility of discredited scholars. The division of Indian history by British historians into Hindu, Muslim and British periods could be notorious, but it continues even today, not because of the British, but because of the redoubtable 'leftism'. They smear ancient India as Hindu period under the belief that a positive appreciation of it is likely to encourage Hindu revivalism as India under Muslim rule can hardly boast of any advancement in any branch of learning and research. They may dub post Harsha period as medieval one, and the earlier one as ancient, but in their inner dialogue they cleanly divide, treat the two as Hindu and Muslim periods, the latter of which has to be blown out of proportion to serve a 'good' cause.

I can go on adding the queries. I feel sorry that academic free for all has become synonymous with Marxism. Marxism is not a dirty, debased, conspiratorial philosophy, fed on lies and half-truths. It is people like Agrawal who have brought Marxism so close to fascism that the boundaries have disappeared. I wish he could learn to understand other's points of view before he took to demolish him. I invite Agrawal and his allies to come out with good defence, to be better Marxists, to write more articles, to think calmly and write and speak with sober head and clear conscience. A false and fabricated history is worse than no history at all.

I recall a journalist who smiled at the simple mention of a review of Dr. Kochhar's book by a highly glamorised historian on ancient India, who managed to control it without knowing the language in which ancient texts are written, in *Frontline* with his one liner 'history Mafia in operation.' For her, all that is knowable was known and written down by the colonial officers, soldiers of Christendom and the rest it being written by their American, German, Scandinavian heirs, she has nothing to bother. The English gone, English is there to salvage her. I do not know whether he shared my inner logic or not. I have no proof that he knew much about history. At first I felt good that a bad review was being adjudged on its merit demerit but then I got dismayed. Any bad comment on a discipline is bad for everyone who associates with it. It was as damaging a comment for me as it was for the reviewer. I, unawares, was as much a part of the Mafia as she was. I brooded to find a breathing hole and convinced myself that everyone who is eager to prove a point, everyone who dilates, distorts, mutilates, subverts, coagulates, inflates or conceals something which he knows to be otherwise is part of a Mafia, either by choice or by design.

Bhagwan Singh